Succeed on the Standardized Test

This Book Includes:

- 2 Summative Assessments (SA)
- Additional practice questions
- Detailed answer explanations for every question
- Type I questions - Concepts, Skills and Procedures
  Type II questions - Expressing Mathematical Reasoning
  Type III questions - Modeling and/or Applications
- Strategies for building speed and accuracy
- Content aligned with the Common Core State Standards

Plus access to Online Workbooks which include:

- Hundreds of practice questions
- Self-paced learning and personalized score reports
- Instant feedback after completion of the workbook

Complement Classroom Learning All Year

Using the Lumos Study Program, parents and teachers can reinforce the classroom learning experience for children. It creates a collaborative learning platform for students, teachers and parents.

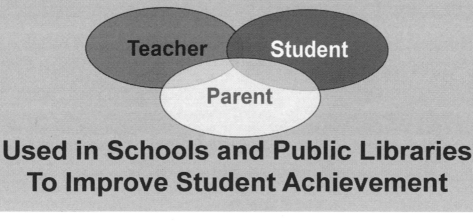

Used in Schools and Public Libraries
To Improve Student Achievement

Lumos Learning

Common Core Assessments and Online Workbooks: Grade 6 Mathematics, PARCC Edition

Contributing Editor	-	**Renee Bade**
Contributing Editor	-	**Gregory Applegate**
Curriculum Director	-	**Marisa Adams**
Executive Producer	-	**Mukunda Krishnaswamy**
Designer and Illustrator	-	**Sowmya R.**

ISBN-10: 1940484219

ISBN-13: 978-1-940484-21-1

Printed in the United States of America

For permissions and additional information contact us

Lumos Information Services, LLC
PO Box 1575, Piscataway, NJ 08855-1575
http://www.LumosLearning.com

Email: support@lumoslearning.com
Tel: (732) 384-0146
Fax: (866) 283-6471

Lumos Learning

Table of Contents

Introduction

The Common Core State Standards Initiative (CCSS) was created from the need to have more robust and rigorous guidelines, which could be standardized from state to state. These guidelines create a learning environment where students will be able to graduate high school with all skills necessary to be active and successful members of society, whether they take a role in the workforce or in some sort of post-secondary education.

Once the CCSS were fully developed and implemented, it became necessary to devise a way to ensure they were assessed appropriately. To this end, states adopting the CCSS have joined one of two consortia, either PARCC or Smarter Balanced.

What is PARCC?

The Partnership for Assessment of Readiness and College and Careers (PARCC) is one of the two state consortiums responsible for developing assessments aligned to the new, more rigorous Common Core State Standards. A combination of educational leaders from PARCC Governing and Participating states, along with test developers, have worked together to create the new computer based English Language Arts and Math Assessments.

PARCC's first round of testing occurred during the 2014-2015 school year. As they remain committed to doing what is best for students, and listening to the parents, educators, and students in the consortium, PARCC worked on a redesign of their test for the following years. They decreased testing time and the amount of tests students would need to take beginning in the 2015-2016 school year.

How Can the Lumos Study Program Prepare Students for PARCC Tests?

At Lumos Learning, we believe that year-long learning and adequate practice before the actual test are the keys to success on these standardized tests. We have designed the Lumos study program to help students get plenty of realistic practice before the test and to promote year-long collaborative learning.

This is a Lumos **tedBook™**. It connects you to Online Workbooks and additional resources using

a number of devices including Android phones, iPhones, tablets and personal computers. The Lumos StepUp Online Workbooks are designed to promote year-long learning. It is a simple program students can securely access using a computer or device with internet access. It consists of hundreds of grade appropriate questions, aligned to the new Common Core State Standards. Students will get instant feedback and can review their answers anytime. Each student's answers and progress can be reviewed by parents and educators to reinforce the learning experience.

How to use this book effectively

The Lumos Program is a flexible learning tool. It can be adapted to suit a student's skill level and the time available to practice before standardized tests. Here are some tips to help you use this book and the online workbooks effectively:

Students

- Take one Summative Assessment (SA).
- Use the "Related Lumos StepUp® Online Workbook" in the Answer Key section to identify the topic that is related to each question.
- Use the Online workbooks to practice your areas of difficulty and complement classroom learning.
- Download the Lumos StepUp® app using the instructions provided in "How can I Download the App" section of this chapter to have anywhere access to online resources.
- Review additional questions in the practice area of the book.
- Take the second Summative Assessment as you get close to the test date.
- Complete the test in a quiet place, following the test guidelines. Practice tests provide you an opportunity to improve your test taking skills and to review topics included in the PARCC test.

Parents

- Familiarize yourself with the PARCC test format and expectations.
- Get useful information about your school by downloading the Lumos SchoolUp™ app. Please follow directions provided in "How to download Lumos SchoolUp™ App" section of this chapter.
- Help your child use Lumos StepUp® Online Workbooks by following the instructions in "How to access the Lumos Online Workbooks" section of this chapter.
- Help your child download the Lumos StepUp® app using the instructions provided in "How can I Download the App" section of this chapter.
- Review your child's performance in the "Lumos Online Workbooks" periodically. You can do this by simply asking your child to log into the system online and selecting the subject area you wish to review.
- Review your child's work in the practice Summative Assessments and Practice Section.

Teachers

- You can use the Lumos online programs along with this book to complement and extend your classroom instruction.

- Get a Free Teacher account by visiting LumosLearning.com/a/stepupbasic

  This Lumos StepUp® Basic account will help you:

  - Create up to 30 student accounts.
  - Review the online work of your students.
  - Easily access CCSS.
  - Create and share information about your classroom or school events.
  - Get insights into students' strengths and weakness in specific content areas.

  NOTE: There is a limit of one grade and subject per teacher for the free account.

- Download the Lumos SchoolUp™ mobile app using the instructions provided in "How can I download the App" section of this chapter.

PARCC Frequently Asked Questions

What Will PARCC Math Assessments Look Like?

In many ways, the PARCC assessments will be unlike anything many students have ever seen. The tests will be conducted online, requiring students complete tasks to assess a deeper understanding of the CCSS. The students will be assessed once 75% of the year has been completed in one Summative based assessment and the Summative Assessment will be broken into four units: Unit 1, Unit 2, Unit 3, and Unit 4.

For Math, PARCC differentiates three different types of questions:

Type I – Tasks assessing concepts, skills, procedures
- Balance of conceptual understanding, fluency, and application
- Can involve any or all mathematical practice standards
- Machine scorable including innovative, computer-based formats

Type II - Tasks assessing expressing mathematical reasoning
- Each task calls for written arguments/justifications, critique of reasoning or precision in mathematical statements.
- Can involve other mathematical practice standards
- May include a mix of machine-scored and hand-scored responses

Type III - Tasks assessing modeling/applications
- Each task calls for modeling/application in a real-world context or scenario
- Can involve other mathematical practice standards
- May include a mix of machine-scored and hand-scored responses

The time for each Math unit is described below:

Estimated Time on Task in Minutes				
Grade	Unit 1	Unit 2	Unit 3	Unit 4
3	60	60	60	60
4	60	60	60	60
5	60	60	60	60
6	80	80	80	80
7	80	80	80	80
8	80	80	80	80

What is a PARCC Aligned Test Practice Book?

Inside this book, you will find two full-length practice tests that are similar to the standardized tests students will take to assess their mastery of CCSS-aligned curriculum. Completing these tests will help students master the different areas that are included in newly aligned standardized tests and practice test taking skills. The results will help the students and educators get insights into students' strengths and weaknesses in specific content areas. These insights could be used to help students strengthen their skills in difficult topics and to improve speed and accuracy while taking the test.

In addition, this book also contains a Practice Session broken into the key types of questions students will see in the four Summative Units: Type I, Type II, and Type III

How is this Lumos tedBook aligned to PARCC Guidelines?

Although the PARCC assessments will be conducted online, the practice tests here have been created to accurately reflect the depth and rigor of PARCC tasks in a pencil and paper format. Students will still be exposed to the TECR technology style questions so they become familiar with the wording and how to think through these types of tasks.

This edition of the practice test book was created in the FALL 2015 and aligned to the most current PARCC standards released to date. Some changes will occur as PARCC continues to release new information in the spring of 2016 and beyond.

How to access the Lumos Online Workbooks

First Time Access:

Using a personal computer with internet access:	Using a smart phone or tablet:
Go to **http://www.lumoslearning.com/book** Enter the following access code in the Access Code field and press the Submit button. Access Code: PG6M-835-27-P **Access Code:** Please enter your Access Code | Submit	Scan the QR Code below and follow the instructions. 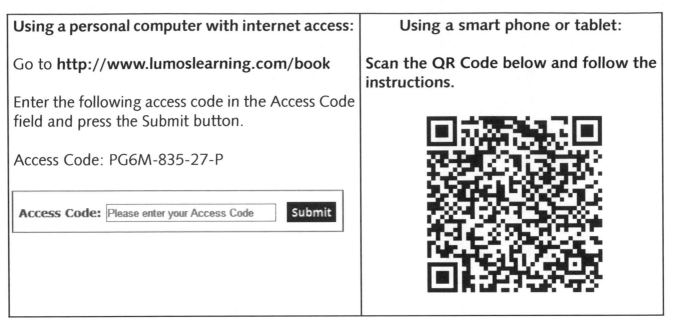

In the next screen, click on the "New User" button to register your user name and password.

> **Login**
> **Lumos Common Core Aligned Online Workbooks - 6th Grade Math**
>
> If you are a New User, please register.
>
> **Login:**
> _____
> **Password:**
> _____
> Enter

Subsequent Access:

After you establish your user id and password for subsequent access, simply login with your account information.

What if I buy more than one Lumos Study Program?

Please note that you can use all Online Workbooks with one User ID and Password. If you buy more than one book, you will access them with the same account.

Go back to the **http://www.lumoslearning.com/book** link and enter the access code provided in the second book. In the next screen simply login using your previously created account.

LumosLearning.com

Lumos StepUp® Mobile App FAQ For Students

What is the Lumos StepUp® App?

It is a FREE application you can download onto your Android smart phones, tablets, iPhones, and iPads.

What are the Benefits of the StepUp® App?

This mobile application gives convenient access to Practice Tests, Common Core State Standards, Online Workbooks, and learning resources through your smart phone and tablet computers.
- Eleven Technology enhanced question types in both MATH and ELA
- Sample questions for Arithmetic drills
- Standard specific sample questions
- Instant access to the Common Core State Standards
- Jokes and cartoons to make learning fun!

Do I Need the StepUp® App to Access Online Workbooks?

No, you can access Lumos StepUp® Online Workbooks through a personal computer. The StepUp® app simply enhances your learning experience and allows you to conveniently access StepUp® Online Workbooks and additional resources through your smart phone or tablet.

How can I Download the App?

Visit **lumoslearning.com/a/stepup-app** using your smart phone or tablet and follow the instructions to download the app.

QR Code
for Smart Phone
Or Tablet Users

Lumos SchoolUp™ Mobile App FAQ For Parents and Teachers

What is the Lumos SchoolUp™ App?

It is a FREE App that helps parents and teachers get a wide range of useful information about their school. It can be downloaded onto smartphones and tablets from popular App Stores.

What are the Benefits of the Lumos SchoolUp™ App?

It provides convenient access to

- School "Stickies". A Sticky could be information about an upcoming test, homework, extra curricular activities and other school events. Parents and educators can easily create their own sticky and share with the school community.
- Common Core State Standards.
- Educational blogs.
- StepUp™ student activity reports.

How can I Download the App?

Visit **lumoslearning.com/a/schoolup-app** using your smartphone or tablet and follow the instructions provided to download the App. Alternatively, scan the QR Code provided below using your smartphone or tablet computer.

**QR Code
for Smart Phone
Or Tablet Users**

LumosLearning.com

Test Taking Tips

1) **The day before the test,** make sure you get a good night's sleep.

2) **On the day of the test,** be sure to eat a good hearty breakfast! Also, be sure to arrive at school on time.

3) **During the test:**

- **Read every question carefully.**
  - Do not spend too much time on any one question. Work steadily through all questions in the section.
  - Attempt all of the questions even if you are not sure of some answers.
  - If you run into a difficult question, eliminate as many choices as you can and then pick the best one from the remaining choices. Intelligent guessing will help you increase your score.
  - Also, make note of the question so that if you have extra time, you can return to it after you reach the end of the section. Try to erase the marks after you complete the work.
  - Some questions may refer to a graph, chart, or other kind of picture. Carefully review the graphic before answering the question.
  - Be sure to include explanations for your written responses and show all work.

- **While Answering Multiple-Choice (EBSR) questions.**
  - Completely fill in the bubble corresponding to your answer choice.
  - Read **all** of the answer choices, even if think you have found the correct answer.

- **While Answering TECR questions.**
  - Read the directions of each question. Some might ask you to drag something, others to select, and still others to highlight. Follow all instructions of the question (or questions if it is in multiple parts)

Summative Assessment (SA) - 1

Student Name: **Start Time:**
Test Date: **End Time:**

Here are some reminders for when you are taking the Grade 6 Mathematics Summative Assessment (SA).

To answer the questions on the test, use the directions given in the question. If you do not know the answer to a question, skip it and go on to the next question. If time permits, you may return to questions in this session only. Do your best to answer every question.

PART - 1

1. The class of 2015 had a dinner fund-raiser and sold "Whole Meal" tickets for $12.00 and "Just Entrée" tickets for $8.00. 240 people attended the event, which cost an average of $10.75 per person.

   Based on this information, write True, False, or Not Enough Information next to each statement below.

Statement	True, False, NEI
More people bought $12.00 tickets.	
More people bought $8.00 tickets.	
The range in price is $4.00.	
Some people bought tickets for $10.75.	

2. Order the following fractions from least to greatest.

   $$\frac{6}{2} \quad \frac{-7}{3} \quad \frac{5}{4} \quad \frac{-1}{3} \quad \frac{4}{3}$$

   Enter your answer in the box.

3.   Guy purchased 48 pencils for $2.40 and Kecia purchased 200 pencils for $6.00.

PART A

Overall, what is the average price the children paid per pencil, to the nearest cent?

Enter your answer in the box.

PART B

Guy and Kecia sold all 248 pencils for $0.25 a piece. How much profit did they make?

Enter your answer in the box.

4.   Find an expression that is equivalent to $2(2x + 6)$.

Select all that apply.

Ⓐ $4x + 6$
Ⓑ $2x + 9 + 2x + 3$
Ⓒ $16x$
Ⓓ $3x + 10 + x + 2$
Ⓔ $4x + 12$

5.   Enter your answer in the box

$10.25 \times 6.2 =$

6.   It took Jin 20 minutes to read 7 pages.

PART A

How many minutes will it take her to complete a 126-page book?

Enter your answer in the box.

Minutes

PART B

If Jin reads for 35 minutes, how many pages did she read?

Enter your answer in the box.

Pages

7. Find the quotient, in simplest form. $\dfrac{5}{6} \div \dfrac{3}{4}$

Enter your answer in the box

8. Which of the following numbers is a solution for the inequality below? {-2, 0, 3, 4, 7}

$$k \geq 3$$

Enter your answer in the box.

9. A movie is rated PG13 meaning that one must be at least 13-years old to watch the movie. The sign in the lobby of the theater reads

> **PG13 Viewers**
> **must be $\leq$ 13**

Nami thinks the sign is wrong, but her friend Tai disagrees and finds nothing wrong with the sign. Who is correct and why?

Enter your answer in the box.

10. **Ryan was talking to his friend Christian, in North Carolina, about the bitter cold weather in Minnesota with a temperature of -17°F. Christian replied, "It's been colder here with temperatures between 13°F and 15°F."**

   <u>**PART A**</u>

   What is wrong with Christian's statement?

   Enter your answer in the box.

   ```




   ```

   <u>**PART B**</u>

   If the temperature in Minnesota rose 20 degrees from -17°F, what would the temperature be? Explain your reasoning.

   Enter your answer in the box.

   ```




   ```

PART - 2

11.   Nico gave Charlie 56 marbles, 40% of Nico's marble collection.

PART A

How many marbles does Nico have remaining?

Enter your answer in the box.

| | Marbles
|-------------------------|

PART B

What is the ratio of marbles between Nico and Charlie in simplest form?

Enter your answer in the box.

PART C

Sebastian has x marbles. If the ratio of marbles between Charlie, and Sebastian is 4 : 5, how many marbles does Sebastian have?

Enter your answer in the box.

| | Marbles
|-------------------------|

12.   Lucy began her climb at 21 feet below sea level and reached an elevation of 1,045 feet above sea level. How many feet did Lucy climb?

Enter your answer in the box.

| | Feet
|-------------------------|

LumosLearning.com   ▲

13. Julia is twice as old as Chen. Chen is x years old and the sum of their ages is 33.

    <u>PART A</u>

    Write an equation to represent this situation.

    Enter your answer in the box.

    <u>PART B</u>

    Use the equation above to solve for Chen and Julia's age.

    Enter your answer in the box.

14. Write an expression for 2 times a number subtracted from 8.

    Enter your answer in the box.

15. Find the area of the triangle in the diagram.

    Enter your answer in the box.

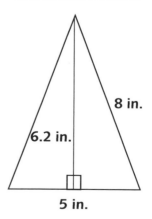

Not drawn to scale

8 in.

6.2 in.

5 in.

16. The table shows the different colors of flowers in Ms. Batiste's garden.

Colors of Flowers	
Color	Number
Pink	20
Yellow	12
Purple	18
White	32

PART A

What is the percentage of pink flowers in her garden?

Enter your answer in the box.

PART B

What is the ratio of pink to yellow to purple to white flowers in simplest form?

Enter your answer in the box.

PART C

If 8 flowers cost $6.99, what is the cost per flower, to the nearest cent?

Enter your answer in the box.

LumosLearning.com

17. The diagram shows a box with a length of $3\frac{1}{3}$ feet, and width of $2\frac{1}{4}$ feet and a height of 4 feet.

PART A

Draw a net to represent this box and label the dimensions with their corresponding measures

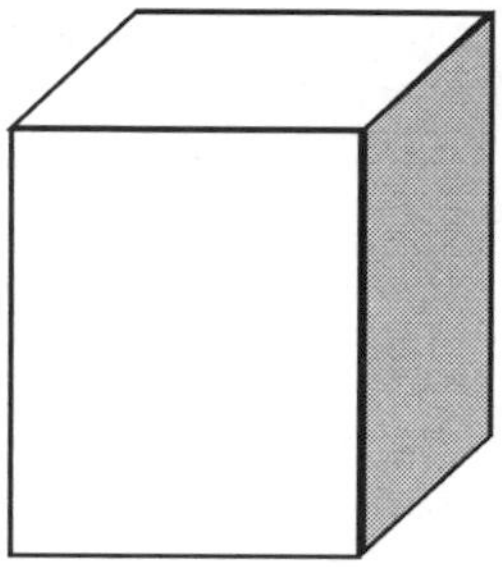

Enter your answer in the box.

PART B

Use the net to calculate the surface area of the box to the nearest foot?

Enter your answer in the box.

18. To qualify for the final race, Tina must have a pace of at most 7.5 minutes per mile in this event.

   ### PART A

   If this event is a 0.6-mile race, write an inequality that represents the time (in minutes), x, that she must complete the race.

   Enter your answer in the box.

   ### PART B

   Use the inequality in Part A to calculate the amount of time in minutes in which Tina could complete this race to qualify for the final race. Represent the solution on the number line provided.

   Enter your answer in the box.

   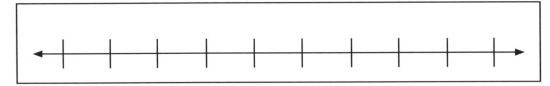

19. The ratio of bluebirds to robins is 3 to 2.

   ### PART A

   Explain what this ratio means.

   Enter your answer in the box.

LumosLearning.com

The teacher asked, "If there is a total of 30 bluebirds and robins, how many bluebirds are there?" Henry answered, "That's easy, 30 divided by 3 is 10." What is inaccurate about his thinking?

Enter your answer in the box.

---

20. George and Maggie were completing their homework together. One problem asked to find the area of a triangle. Below are George's and Maggie's work.

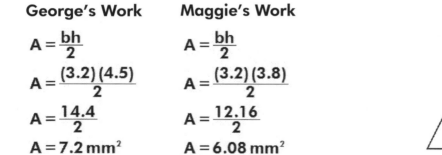
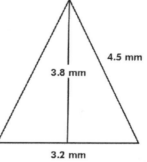

George's Work

$$A = \frac{bh}{2}$$

$$A = \frac{(3.2)(4.5)}{2}$$

$$A = \frac{14.4}{2}$$

$$A = 7.2 \text{ mm}^2$$

Maggie's Work

$$A = \frac{bh}{2}$$

$$A = \frac{(3.2)(3.8)}{2}$$

$$A = \frac{12.16}{2}$$

$$A = 6.08 \text{ mm}^2$$

4.5 mm
3.8 mm
3.2 mm

Whose answer is correct? Explain your reasoning.

Enter your answer in the box.

PART - 3

21. Which of the following is a statistical question?

   (A) How many students have blue eyes?
   (B) What are the ages of the people who attended the concert?
   (C) How much older is Kierra than Garrett?
   (D) How many days did it snow in January?

22. What is the greatest common factor of 24 and 96?

   Enter your answer in the box.

23. What is 5 · 5 · 5 · 5 · 5 · 5 · 5 written in exponential form?

   Enter your answer in the box.

24. How many $\frac{1}{3}$ inch cubes will fit in the box shown in the diagram?
   (Cubes cannot be cut apart.)

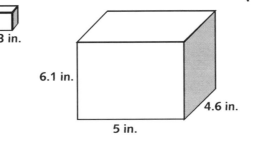

1/3 in.

6.1 in.

4.6 in.

5 in.

   Enter your answer in the box.

25. Ambry ran a 3.1-mile race in 18 minutes.

   ## PART A

   What is Ambry's average pace in minutes per mile, to the nearest hundredth?

   Enter your answer in the box.

   ## PART B

   If Ambry ran a marathon, which is 26.2 miles, at this same pace, how many minutes would it take him to complete the marathon, to the nearest minute?

   Enter your answer in the box.

LumosLearning.com

26. Mario bought gas for $4.30 per gallon.

PART A

If his car took $8^{1/2}$ gallons of gas, how much did he spend on gas?

Enter your answer in the box.

	$

PART B

The next week Mario bought gas again at the same price per gallon and spent $88.58. How many gallons of gas did he get?

Enter your answer in the box.

	Gallons

27. A survey was conducted on the ages of the visitors to the county fair. The data from the first 30 visitors surveyed is tabulated below. Use the grid provided to draw a histogram of this data. Be sure to include a title for the graph, label the axes, and select an appropriate scale.

Ages of Fair Visitors	
Age Range	Number of people
1 - 20 years	10
21 - 40 years	12
41 - 60 years	7
61 - 80 years	1

1-20 years	21-40 years	41-60 years	61-80 years

28. James counted the number of trucks he saw on his way to school for 10 days. Below is the data he collected.

$$10, 8, 20, 15, 16, 9, 10, 24, 18, 19$$

PART A

Determine the median, first quartile and third quartile for this set of data.

Enter your answer in the box.

PART B

Use the above information and create a box-and-whisker plot of the data.

Enter your answer in the box.

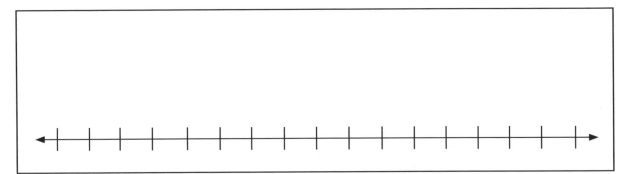

29. The diagram to the right models $\frac{2}{3} \div \frac{1}{6}$ showing that there are four $\frac{1}{6}$th pieces in $\frac{2}{3}$rds of a piece.

PART A

What is $\frac{3}{4} \div \frac{1}{8}$?

Enter your answer in the box.

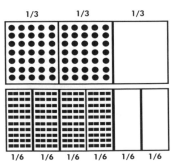

LumosLearning.com

PART B

Draw a diagram to model $\frac{3}{4} \div \frac{1}{8}$.

Enter your answer in the box.

30. The ratio of dogs to cats in a certain neighborhood is 5 to 2.

   ## PART A

   If there are 45 dogs in the neighborhood, how many cats are there? Show or explain how you arrived at your answer.

   Enter your answer in the box.

   ## PART B

   If two families move out of the neighborhood and take with them three dogs and no cats, what is the new ratio of dogs to cats?

   Enter your answer in the box.

PART - 4

31. Isabella recorded the inches of rain per month for twelve months.

     7, 8, 11, 12, 17, 18, 18, 15, 11, 9, 10, 6

    ### PART A

    Determine the median, first quartile and third quartile for this set of data.

    Enter your answer in the box.

    ┌───┐
    │   │
    │   │
    │   │
    └───┘

    ### PART B

    Use the above information and create a box-plot of the data.

    Enter your answer in the box.

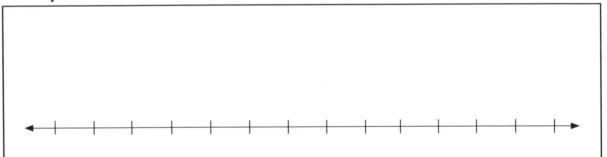

32. What is the value of the following expression when p = 3, q = 10, r = 3 and s=16

    $$\frac{p^2 + 2q + 18 \div r}{s}$$

    Enter your answer in the box. ┌────────────────────────────┐
                                    │   │
                                    └────────────────────────────┘

33. Andrea is planning a party for her younger brother. She received invitation replies that included 4 adults, 2 senior adults, and 35 children.

PART A

Using the information in the table, write an expression to represent the amount of money needed for the movie tickets.

Enter your answer in the box.

[   ]

Tickets Costs

Age	Cost
Seniors	$8.50
Adults	$14.00
Children	$11.50

PART B

Using the expression above, calculate the cost of the movie tickets.

Enter your answer in the box. [   ]

34. Noah's soccer team played 12 games and won 10 of these.

PART A

What is the ratio of wins to losses?

Enter your answer in the box. [   ]

PART B

What is the percentage of the games won?

Enter your answer in the box. [   ]

PART C

If they only win one of the next three games, what is the new ratio of wins to losses?

Enter your answer in the box. [   ]

35. $79{,}744 \div 356 =$

Enter your answer in the box.

36. It takes Zoe 3 minutes to paint one fingernail.

PART A

Write an equation that shows the time, *t*, it takes to paint *f* fingernails.

Enter your answer in the box.

PART B

How many minutes will it take Zoe to paint 50 fingernails?

Enter your answer in the box.

PART C

Convert the minutes in Part B to hours.

Enter your answer in the box.

37. Locate $\dfrac{-1}{4}$ on the number line.

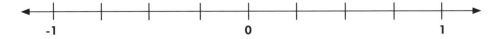

38. Mrs. Jackson is planning an outdoor barbeque. She will cook 2 ears of corn per person plus two extra.

PART A

If 16 people plan to come, how many ears of corn will Mrs. Jackson cook?

Enter your answer in the box.

Ears of corn

PART B

Show or explain how you arrived at your answer.

Enter your answer in the box.

End of Summative Assessment (SA) - 1

Summative Assessment (SA) - 1

Answer Key

Question No.	Answer	Related Lumos Online Workbook	CCSS
PART - 1			
1	*	Distribution	6.SP.2
2	*	Absolute Value	6.NS.7
3 Part A	$0.03	Unit Rates	6.RP.2
3 Part B	$53.60	Solving One-Step Equations	6.EE.7
4	*	Identifying Equivalent Expressions; Writing Equivalent Expressions	6.EE.4, 6.EE.3
5	63.55	Operations with Decimals	6.NS.3
6 Part A	360	Unit Rates	6.RP.2
6 Part B	$12^{1/4}$ pages	Solving Real World Ratio Problems	6.RP.3
7	1 1/9	Division of Fractions	6.NS.1
8	3, 4, 7	Equations and Inequalities	6.EE.5
9	*	Representing Inequalities	6.EE.8
10 Part A	*	Absolute Value	6.NS.7B
10 Part B	3°F	Absolute Value	6.NS.7B
PART - 2			
11 Part A	84 marbles	Solving Real World Ratio Problems	6.RP.3C
11 Part B	3:2	Expressing Ratios	6.RP.1
11 Part C	70 marbles	Expressing Ratios	6.RP.1
12	1,066 ft.	Positive and Negative Numbers	6.NS.5
13 Part A	x + 2x = 33 or 3x = 33	Solving One-Step Equations	6.EE.7
13 Part B	11 and 22 years	Solving One-Step Equations	6.EE.7
14	8 - 2x	Expressions Involving Variables	6.EE.2A
15	15 1/2 inches^2	Area	6.G.1

* See detailed explanation

     LumosLearning.com   ▲

Question No.	Answer	Related Lumos Online Workbook	CCSS
16 Part A	24%	Solving Real World Ratio Problems	6.RP.3C
16 Part B	10 : 6 : 9 : 16	Using Common Factors	6.NS.4
16 Part C	$0.87	Solving Real World Ratio Problems	6.RP.3B
17 Part A	*	Nets	6.G.4
17 Part B	59 2/3 ft²	Nets	6.G.4
18 Part A	x≤7.5 × 0.6	Representing Inequalities	6.EE.8
18 Part B	*	Representing Inequalities	6.EE.8
19 Part A	3:2	Expressing Ratios	6.RP.1
19 Part B	*	Expressing Ratios	6.RP.1
20	*	Area	6.G.1
PART - 3			
21	B	Statistical Questions	6.SP.1
22	24	Using Common Factors	6.NS.4
23	5⁷	Whole Number Exponents	6.EE.1
24	3,510 cubes	Surface Area and Volume	6.G.2
25 Part A	5.81 minutes per mile	Unit Rates	6.RP.2
25 Part B	152 minutes	Unit Rates	6.RP.2
26 Part A	$36.55	Solving Real World Ratio Problems	6.RP.3
26 Part B	20.6 gallons	Solving Real World Ratio Problems	6.RP.3
27	*	Graphs and Charts	6.SP.4
28 Part A	*	Graphs and Charts	6.SP.4
28 Part B	*	Graphs and Charts	6.SP.4
29 Part A	6	Division of Fractions	6.NS.1
29 Part B	*	Division of Fractions	6.NS.1
30 Part A	*	Solving Real World Ratio Problems	6.RP.3
30 Part B	*	Solving Real World Ratio Problems	6.RP.3
PART - 4			
31 Part A	*	Graphs and Charts	6.SP.4
31 Part B	*	Graphs and Charts	6.SP.4
32	2 3/16	Expressions Involving Variables	6.EE.2C

* See detailed explanation

Question No.	Answer	Related Lumos Online Workbook	CCSS
33 Part A	*	Whole Number Exponents	6.EE.1
33 Part B	$475.50	Whole Number Exponents	6.EE.1
34 Part A	5 : 1	Expressing Ratios	6.RP.1
34 Part B	83%	Solving Real World Ratio Problems	6.RP.3C
34 Part C	11:4	Expressing Ratios	6.RP.1
35	224	Division of Whole Numbers	6.NS.2
36 Part A	3f = t	Quantitative Relationships	6.EE.9
36 Part B	150 minutes	Expressions Involving Variables	6.EE.2C
36 Part C	2.5 hours	Solving Real World Ratio Problems	6.RP.3D
37	*	Representing Negative Numbers	6.NS.6A
38 Part A	34 ears of corn	Solving Real World Ratio Problems	6.RP.3
38 Part B	*	Solving Real World Ratio Problems	6.RP.3

* See detailed explanation

▲

Summative Assessment (SA) - 1

Detailed Explanations

Question No.	Answer	Detailed Explanation

<table>
<tr><td colspan="3" align="center">PART - 1</td></tr>
</table>

1

Statement	True / False NEI
More people bought $12.00 tickets.	True - $10.75 is closer to 12 than it is to $8.00
More people bought $8.00 tickets.	False - $10.75 is farther away from $8.00 than it is from $12.00
The range in price is $4.00.	True - $12.00 - $8.00 = $4.00
Some people bought tickets for $10.75.	False – Only $8.00 and $12.00 tickets were sold.

2

When ordering fractions with different denominators, first get a common denominator. In this case, 12 is the least common denominator.

$$\frac{36}{12} \cdot \frac{28}{12} \quad \frac{15}{12} \cdot \frac{4}{12} \quad \frac{16}{12}$$

Then order the numerators from least to greatest and rewrite the fractions in their original form.

$$-\frac{28}{12} \cdot \frac{4}{12} \quad \frac{15}{12} \quad \frac{16}{12} \quad \frac{36}{12} \rightarrow -\frac{7}{3}, \ -\frac{1}{2}, \ \frac{5}{4}, \ \frac{4}{3}, \ \frac{6}{2}$$

3 Part A — $.03

To obtain the average price per pencil, divide the total amount paid by the total number of pencils purchased. Then round to the nearest cent (hundredth).

$$\frac{\$2.40 + \$6.00}{48 + 200} = \frac{\$8.40}{248} = \$.03$$

3 Part B — $53.60

To find how much profit was made, calculate the money earned from the sale and subtract the cost of the pencils.

$$(248 \times \$0.25) - (\$2.40 + \$6.00) = \$62.00 - \$8.40 = \$53.60$$

4 — B, D and E

B) $2x + 9 + 2x + 3$ - when like terms are combined this is equivalent to $4x + 12$
D) $3x + 10 + x + 2$ - when like terms are combined this is equivalent to $4x + 12$
E) $4x + 12$ – this is the answer in simplest form

Question No.	Answer	Detailed Explanation
5	63.55	$10.25 \times 6.2 = 63.55$
6 Part A	360 minutes	Since you know the ratio of minutes to pages, set up a proportion and solve. $\dfrac{20\ \text{minutes}}{7\ \text{pages}} = \dfrac{x\ \text{minutes}}{126\ \text{pages}}\ ; (20)(126) = 7x;\ 2520 = 7x\ ;\ 360 = x$ It will take Jin 360 minutes to complete a 126-page book.
6 Part B	12¼ pages	If it takes Jin 20 minutes to read 7 pages, you can set up a proportion to solve for the number of pages she can read in 35 minutes. $\dfrac{20\ \text{minutes}}{7\ \text{pages}} = \dfrac{35\ \text{minutes}}{x\ \text{pages}}\ ; 20x = (7)(35)\ ; 20x = 245\ ; 12.25 = x$ Jin can read $12\dfrac{1}{4}$ pages in 35 minutes.
7	1 1/9	Dividing by a fraction is the same as multiplying by its reciprocal. $\dfrac{5}{6} \div \dfrac{3}{4} = \dfrac{5}{6} \times \dfrac{4}{3} = \dfrac{20}{18} = 1\dfrac{2}{18} = 1\dfrac{1}{9}$
8	3, 4, 7	{3, 4, 7} $k \geq 3$ means a number k must be greater than or equal to 3. Of the numbers in the set {-2, 0, 3, 4, 7} only 3, 4, and 7 are greater than or equal to 3. Thus, these are the only solutions to the inequality found in this set.
9	Nami	Nami is correct, the sign is wrong. To be at least 13 years old means to be 13 years old or older. Hence the correct inequality symbol is $\geq$ and not $\leq$. The arrow points toward the smaller number. In this case the small number is 13.
10 Part A		-17°F is 17 degrees below 0°F whereas 13°F is 13 degrees above 0 and 15°F is 15 degrees above 0. So -17°F is 30°F colder than 13°F.
10 Part B	3°F	$-17 + 20 = 3°F$
	PART - 2	
11 Part A	84 marbles	To find the number or marbles Nico has left, first find out how much he started with by finding 40% of what number is 56. $40\% \times x = 56\ ; x = \dfrac{56}{40\%}\ ; \dfrac{56}{.40}\ ; 140\ \text{marbles}$ If Nico has 140 marbles and gave 56 to Charlie, he now has 140 – 56 or 84 marbles.

     LumosLearning.com

Question No.	Answer	Detailed Explanation
11 Part B	3:2	In Part A, you determined the number of marbles Nico has is 84. Compare 84 and 56 in a ratio and simplify. $$\frac{84}{56} \div \frac{2}{2} = \frac{42}{28} \div \frac{2}{2} = \frac{21}{14} \div \frac{7}{7} = \frac{3}{2}; 3:2$$
11 Part C	70 marbles	Compare the ratio of 4 : 5 to the ratio of the actual number of marbles. $4:5 = 56:x$. Set up equivalent ratios $\frac{4}{5} = \frac{56}{x}$ $$\frac{4}{5} = \frac{56}{x}; 4x = (56)(5); 4x = 280; x = 70 \text{ marbles}$$
12	1,066 feet.	Note that Lucy begins her climb below sea level or below 0 feet. She must climb 21 feet to get to 0 feet and then climb an additional 1,045 feet. The total number of feet she climbed is 21 + 1,045 or 1,066 feet.
13 Part A		If Chen is x years old, Julia is $2x$ years old. If the sum of their ages is 33 the following equation can be written. $x + 2x = 33$ or $3x = 33$
13 Part B		$x + 2x = 33$; $3x = 33$; $x = 11$ - Chen is 11 years old. $2(11) = 22$ – Julia is 22 years old.
14	$8 - 2x$	Be careful with the phase "subtracted from". This means that $2x$ is subtracted from 8. $8 - 2x$
15	$15\frac{1}{2}$ inches²	The area of a triangle is calculated using the formula $A_{triangle} = \dfrac{base \times height}{2}$. The base must be perpendicular, form a 90° angle, to the height. In this diagram the base is 5-in and the height is 6.2-in. $$A = \frac{5 \times 6.2}{2} = \frac{31}{2} = 15\frac{1}{2} \text{ inches}^2$$
16 Part A	24%	Find the fraction of pink flowers to all flowers and then write it has a percent.
16 Part B	10:6:9: 16	The ratio of pink to yellow to purple to white flowers is 20:12:18:32. To write this in simplest form, find the greatest common factor and divide each number by that factor. 20: 1, 2, 4, 5, 10, 20 12: 1,2,3,4,6,12 18: 1,2,3,6,9,18 32: 1,2,4,8,16,32 The greatest common factor is 2 so the simplify ratio is 10:6:9:16

Question No.	Answer	Detailed Explanation
16 Part C	$0.87	If 8 flowers cost $6.99 then divide $6.99 by 8 to get the cost of one flower.
17 Part A		
17 Part B	59 2/3 ft²	Find the surface area by summing the area of all the surfaces. $$2\left(3\tfrac{1}{3}\times 4\right)+2\left(3\tfrac{1}{3}\times 2\tfrac{1}{4}\right)+2\left(4\times 2\tfrac{1}{4}\right)=2\left(\tfrac{10}{3}\times\tfrac{4}{1}\right)+2\left(\tfrac{10}{3}\times\tfrac{9}{4}\right)+2\left(\tfrac{4}{1}\times\tfrac{9}{4}\right)$$ $$=2\left(\tfrac{40}{3}\right)+2\left(\tfrac{90}{12}\right)+2(9)$$ $$\left(\tfrac{80}{3}\right)+\left(\tfrac{180}{12}\right)+18=59\tfrac{2}{3}\ \text{ft}^2$$
18 Part A	x≤7.5× 0.6	Multiply Tina's pace by 0.6 to find the time she must beat. $$x\le 7.5\times 0.6$$
18 Part B		0< x≤4.5 Tina must complete the race in at most 4.5 minutes to qualify for the final event.
19 Part A	3:2	A ratio of bluebirds to robins of 3: 2 means that for every 3 bluebirds there are two robins.
19 Part B		In a ratio of 3 to 2 there are a total of 5 parts. This means one part out of a total of 30 is 30 ÷ 5 or 6 birds. If three parts are bluebirds then 3 × 6 or 18 are blue birds. Henry divided the total of 30 by 3 parts, which is incorrect.
20	Maggie's answer is correct	Maggie's answer is correct. The height of a triangle is perpendicular to its base. George used the side of the triangle as the triangle's height but the side is not perpendicular to the base of 3.2mm. Maggie, however, did use the height, which is 3.8 mm, as it is perpendicular to the base.

LumosLearning.com   ▲

Question No.	Answer	Detailed Explanation
		PART - 3
21	B	Of all the questions B is the only one that has an answer with variation. The ages of the people who attended the concert will vary. The answers to questions A, C and D result in a single number answer.
22	24	Write the factors of each number and determine the greatest one they have in common. 24: 1, 2, 3, 4, 6, 8, 12, 24 96: 1, 2, 3, 4, 6, 8, 12, 16, 24, 32, 48, 96 The greatest factor in common is 24.
23	5^7	To write in exponential form, the base is the number being multiplied and the exponent is the number of times it is being multiplied.
24	3,510 cubes	Find the number of 1/3 in. cubes that will fit along the length, width, and height of the box. $$5 \div \frac{1}{3} = \frac{5}{1} \times \frac{3}{1} = 15 \text{ cubes}$$ $$4.6 \div \frac{1}{3} = \frac{4.6}{1} \times \frac{3}{1} = 13.8 \text{ cubes or 13 cubes}$$ $$6.1 \div \frac{1}{3} = \frac{6.1}{1} \times \frac{3}{1} = 18.3 \text{ cubes or 18 cubes}$$ Then use the volume formula for a rectangular prism to find the total number of cubes the box will hold. $V = l \times w \times h = 15 \times 13 \times 18 = 3,510$ cubes
25 Part A	5.81	Use the words in the problem to help solve the problem. Minutes per mile means $\frac{\text{minutes}}{\text{miles}}$ $$\frac{18 \text{ minutes}}{3.1 \text{ miles}} = \frac{x \text{ minutes}}{1 \text{ miles}} ; (18)(1) = 3.1x ; 5.81 = x.$$ Ambry can run 5.81 minutes per mile.
25 Part B	152 minutes	In Part A, you found how fast Ambry could run 1 mile. If you multiply this pace by the number of miles, 26.2, you will determine the amount of time it will take to complete a marathon. $$26.2 \text{ mile} \times \frac{5.81 \text{ minutes}}{1 \text{ mile}} = 152.222 \text{ minutes or 152 minutes}$$
26 Part A	$36.55	Since you know the price per gallon, multiply it by the number of gallons to determine the total cost. $$\$4.30 \times 8\frac{1}{2} = \$4.30 \times 8.5 = \$36.55$$

Question No.	Answer	Detailed Explanation

27

28 Part A

Order the numbers: 8, 9, 10, 10, 15, 16, 18, 19, 20, 24
Find the median: 8, 9, 10, 10, 15, 16, 18, 19, 20, 24 = 15.5
Find Q1, the median of the first half of the data: 8, 9, 10, 10, 15 = 10
Find Q3, the median of the second half of the data: 16, 18, 19, 20, 24 = 19

28 Part B

29 Part A and B **6**

30 Part A

Question No.	Answer	Detailed Explanation
30 Part B		There are now 45 − 3 or 42 dogs and 18 cats. The GCF between 42 and 18 is 6, so now for every 7 dogs there are 3 cats.

$$\frac{42}{18} \div \frac{6}{6} = \frac{7}{3}$$

Dogs
6 groups of 7 = 42

Cats
6 groups of 3 = 18

7

3

PART - 4

31 Part A

Order the numbers: 6, 7, 8, 9, 10, 11, 11, 12, 15, 17, 18, 18

Find the median: 6, 7, 8, 9, 10, 11, 11, 12, 15, 17, 18, 18 = 11

Find Q1, the median of the first half of the data: 6, 7, 8, 9, 10, 11 = 8.5

Find Q3, the median of the second half of the data: 11, 12, 15, 17, 18, 18 = 16

31 Part B

| 32 | $2\frac{3}{16}$ | Substitute the values for each variable and solve paying close attention to the order of operations. |

$$\frac{p^2 + 2q + 18 \div r}{s} = \frac{3^2 + 2(10) + 18 \div 3}{16} = \frac{9 + 2(10) + 18 \div 3}{16}$$

$$= \frac{9 + 20 + 18 \div 3}{16} = \frac{9 + 20 + 18 \div 3}{16} = \frac{9 + 20 + 6}{16} = \frac{35}{16} = 2\frac{3}{16}$$

33 Part A		2($8.50) + 4($14.00) + 35($11.50) = M
33 Part B	$475.50	2($8.50) + 4($14.00) + 35($11.50) = $17.00 + $56.00 + $402.50 = $475.50
34 Part A	5:1	If Noah's team won 10 games then they lost 2 games. The ratio of wins to losses is 10 : 2 or 5 : 1.

Question No.	Answer	Detailed Explanation
34 Part B	83%	Write the fraction of games won and convert to a percent. $$\frac{10}{12} = 0.83\,;0.83 \times 100 = 83\%$$
34 Part C	11:4	After these three games they would have 10 + 1 or 11 wins and 2 + 2 or 4 losses. The ratio of wins to losses is now 11: 4.
35	224	$79{,}744 \div 356 = 224$
36 Part A	3f = t	$3f = t$
36 Part B	150 minutes	Substitute 50 for f in the equation in PART A. $3(50) = 150$ minutes
36 Part C	2.5 hours	There are 60 minutes to an hour, so divide 150 minutes by 60 minutes. $$150\ mins \times \frac{1\,hours}{60\,minutes} = 2.5\,hours$$
37		
38 Part A	34 ears of corn	
38 Part B		I let x equal the number of people attending the barbeque. Then I multiplied the number of people by 2, because each person gets two ears of corn. Then I add 2 to this product for the two extra ears of corn. The expression I used was 2x + 2. $2(16) + 2 = 32 + 2 = 34$ ears of corn

LumosLearning.com

Summative Assessment (SA) - 2

Student Name:
Test Date:

Start Time:
End Time:

Here are some reminders for when you are taking the Grade 6 Mathematics Summative Assessment (SA).

To answer the questions on the test, use the directions given in the question. If you do not know the answer to a question, skip it and go on to the next question. If time permits, you may return to questions in this session only. Do your best to answer every question.

PART - 1

1. Caleb is creating a portion of a basketball court in his driveway as shown in the diagram. The symbol ′ means feet and ″ means inches. 18′ 9″ means 18 feet and 9 inches.

PART A

Convert 18 feet 9 inches to feet only.

Enter your answer in the box.

Feet

PART B

What is the area of the rectangular region, in square feet?

Enter your answer in the box.

Feet²

PART C

What is the area of the semicircular region? Use 3.14 for π.

Enter your answer in the box.

Feet²

PART D

What is the perimeter, outline in dotted line above, of the portion of the basketball court Caleb is creating? Use 3.14 for π.

Enter your answer in the box.

LumosLearning.com

2. The band is collecting soup can labels as a fund-raiser. The number of soup cans collected by each of the 10 members is listed below.

40, 14, 36, 19, 32, 26, 4, 15, 26, 38

Based on this information, write **True, False, or Not Enough Information** next to each statement below.

Statement	True, False, NEI
The mean is less than the mode.	
The median and the mode are equal.	
The mode is the middle number.	
If Charlotte brought in 10 instead of 4, the median would be greater.	

3. To qualify for the Olympic marathon trials, men must run 2:18, 2 hours and 18 minutes, or faster, and women must run 2:43 or faster?

PART A

Write two inequalities, one to represent the women's, w, and one to represent the men's, m, qualifying times.

Enter your answer in the box.

PART B

Based on the information in the table, write the names of those who qualify for the 2016 Olympic marathon trials.

Name	Gender	Time
Emilio	M	2:16
Alma	F	2:46
Hailey	F	2:43
Oliver	M	2:19
Isaiah	M	2:21
Tiana	F	2:40

Enter your answer in the box.

```
┌─────────────────────────────────────────────────────┐
│                                                       │
│                                                       │
│                                                       │
│                                                       │
└─────────────────────────────────────────────────────┘
```

4. Order the following numbers from least to greatest.

$$0.75 \quad \frac{8}{6} \quad -50\% \quad \frac{-15}{3} \quad 0.7$$

Enter your answer in the box.

```
┌─────────────────────────────────────────────────────┐
│                                                       │
│                                                       │
│                                                       │
│                                                       │
│                                                       │
└─────────────────────────────────────────────────────┘
```

5. Mr. Sydow bought ice cream sandwiches for the softball team.

    PART A

    If there are 20 team members and it cost Mr. Sydow $35.80, how much does it cost for one ice cream sandwich?

    Enter your answer in the box.

```
┌─────────────────────────────────────────────────────┐
│                                                       │
│                                                       │
│                                                       │
│                                                       │
│                                                       │
└─────────────────────────────────────────────────────┘
```

    PART B

    Coach Griffin offered to buy ice cream sandwiches for all 28 members of the baseball team. How much will Mr. Griffin have to pay?

    Enter your answer in the box.

```
┌─────────────────────────────────────────────────────┐
│                                                       │
│                                                       │
│                                                       │
│                                                       │
└─────────────────────────────────────────────────────┘
```

LumosLearning.com   ▼

6. Find an expression that is equivalent to -3(4x - 6).

   Select all that apply.

   Ⓐ   -10x + 7 – 2x + 11
   Ⓑ   x - 3
   Ⓒ   6x
   Ⓓ   -12x + 18
   Ⓔ   -12 x - 6

7. What is the value of $\dfrac{7}{8} \div \dfrac{5}{6}$ in simplest form?

   Enter your answer in the box.

8. The diagram shows a net of a 3D figure.

   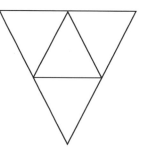

   PART A

   What figure does this net represent? Be specific.

   Enter your answer in the box.

Each of the triangles is equilateral with a height of 6.9-in and sides of 8-in, what is the surface area of the net?

Enter your answer in the box.

9. The class was asked to graph the inequality of "at most 20" on a number line. Below is Landon's graph.

20

Is Landon's graph correct? Explain your reasoning

Enter your answer in the box.

10. Tristan's father was at the store looking at carpet for the dining room. He called Tristan and asked him how much carpet was needed. Tristan said he would call back with the measurement. Below is Tristan's work.

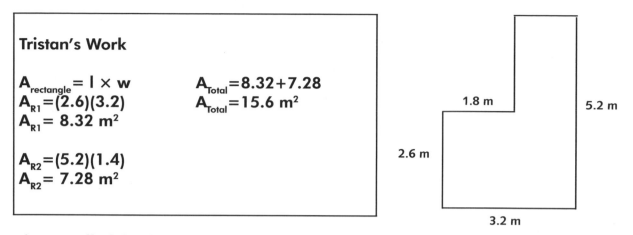

Tristan's Work

$A_{rectangle} = l \times w$ $A_{Total} = 8.32 + 7.28$
$A_{R1} = (2.6)(3.2)$ $A_{Total} = 15.6 \ m^2$
$A_{R1} = 8.32 \ m^2$

$A_{R2} = (5.2)(1.4)$
$A_{R2} = 7.28 \ m^2$

1.8 m
5.2 m
2.6 m
3.2 m

Tristan called back and told his father 16 square meters. Do you agree with Tristan? Explain your reasoning.

Enter your answer in the box.

PART - 2

11. **25.745 ÷ 0.005 =**

Enter your answer in the box.

[ ]

12. **Aki walks 1.6 kilometers to school in 20 minutes.**

PART A

At this rate, how many minutes would it take her to walk 900 meters?

Enter your answer in the box.

[ ] Minutes

PART B

If Aki walks for 72 minutes, how far would she walk, in kilometers?

Enter your answer in the box.

[ ] Kilometers

13. **During a camping trip, Nathan, Brandon and Chet had a firefly catching contest. Nathan caught three for every five Brandon caught and every four Chet caught.**

PART A

If they caught 60 fireflies all together, how many did Brandon catch?

Enter your answer in the box.

[ ] Fireflies

         ▼

PART B

How many more fireflies did Chet catch than Nathan?

Enter your answer in the box.

	Fireflies

PART C

If Brandon catches 5 more fireflies, what is the new firefly ratio between Brandon and Chet, in simplest form?

Enter your answer in the box.

	Fireflies

14. Maya opened a checking account and deposited $250.00. If she now has an account balance of

    -12.50, how much did she withdraw?

PART A

Enter your answer in the box.

	$

PART B

What does an account balance of -12.50 mean?

Enter your answer in the box.

15. Write an expression for 5 less than 3 times a number.

Enter your answer in the box.

```


```

16. Find the area of the pentagon in the diagram.

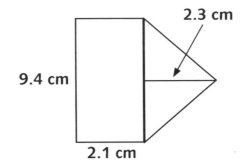

Enter your answer in the box.

```



```

17. Addison went to the amusement park at the fair.

PART A

In order to ride the Astro Blaster ride, Addison must be at least 54 inches tall. Addison is 45 inches tall. Write an inequality to represent how much taller, h, Addison must be to ride the Astro Blaster.

Enter your answer in the box.

```


```

PART B

Use the inequality in PART A to calculate how much taller Addison must be to ride the Astro Blaster?

Enter your answer in the box.

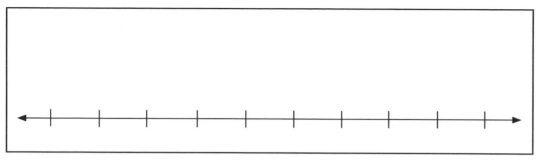

18.   Liwei is selling two golf balls for $1.00.

PART A

Complete the table based on the information above.

Dollars	1.00		3.00		5.00
Golf Balls		4		8	

PART B

Write an equation to express golf balls, g, in terms of dollars, d.

PART C

If Liwei receives $54.00, how many golf balls did he sell?

Golf Balls

19. A box of 500 envelopes costs $14.89. Before buying, Mr. Ruiz wants to know the price for one envelope. His son Alan quickly makes a calculation and says, "You can buy almost 34 envelopes for $1.00." Here is Alan's work.

$$\frac{500}{\$14.89} \div \frac{\$14.89}{\$14.89} = \frac{33.6}{\$1.00}$$

Mr. Ruiz thanked his son, but said that was not the answer he was looking for.

PART A

What is the cost for one envelope?

Enter your answer in the box.

PART B

Explain how Alan misunderstood his father's request.

Enter your answer in the box.

LumosLearning.com

20. The third grade class took a field trip to the zoo. Several of the students counted their favorite animals. Below is a table of the data they collected.

Animal	Count
Tigers	10
Zebras	8
Monkeys	22
Ostriches	16
Pandas	4
Koala Bears	6

PART A

Determine the median for this set of data.

Enter your answer in the box.

PART B

Use the grid provided to draw a bar graph of this data. Be sure to include a title for the graph, label the axes, and select an appropriate scale.

Enter your answer in the box.

PART - 3

21.   The table shows the different baked goods sold by the Consumer Science Club.

Colors of Flowers	
Baked Good	**Cost**
Rice Krispies® Treats	$0.50
Granola Clusters	$0.25
Fruit Tart	$1.50
Fudge Brownie	$2.25

PART A

What is the cost ratio between a Rice Krispies® treat and a fruit tart, in simplest form?

Enter your answer in the box.

PART B

To sell the fudge brownies faster, the price was changed to 3 for $5.00. What is the new unit price per brownie, to the nearest cent?

Enter your answer in the box.

$/brownie

PART C

Imani bought 4 Rice Krispies® treats, 4 granola clusters, and 2 fruit tarts to share with friends. What percentage of the total cost was spent on fruit tarts?

Enter your answer in the box.

	%

22. **Which of the following is a statistical question?**

Select all that apply.

Ⓐ What is the life span of a dog?
Ⓑ How many days in a week?
Ⓒ How many players are on your team?
Ⓓ How many gallons of fuel does it take to drive a mile?

23. **Which expression is equivalent to 15 + 6?**

Ⓐ 3(12 + 3)
Ⓑ 5(3 + 6)
Ⓒ 3(5 + 2)
Ⓓ 5(15 + 1)

24. **What is the value of $3^2 - 2^3 + 4^2$?**

Enter your answer in the box.

25. How many $\frac{1}{4}$ cm cubes will fit in the box shown in the diagram?

Note - Cubes cannot be cut apart.

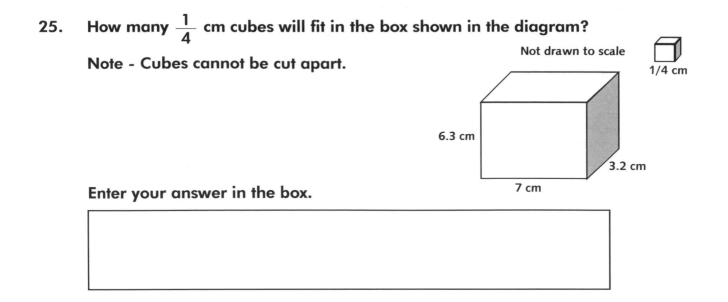

Not drawn to scale

1/4 cm

6.3 cm

3.2 cm

7 cm

Enter your answer in the box.

26. Sean Wrona is the fastest typist in the world and can type an average of about 500 words in three minutes.

PART A

What is Sean's average typing speed in words per minute, WPM, to the nearest whole number?

Enter your answer in the box.

WPM

PART B

How long will it take Sean to type a 2,380-word document, to the nearest tenth of a minute?

Enter your answer in the box.

minutes

LumosLearning.com

27. Chloe picked x quarts of blueberries. Avery picked 3 quarts less than Chloe. Together they picked 9 quarts of blueberries.

PART A

Write an equation to represent this situation.

Enter your answer in the box.

```



```

PART B

Use the equation above to solve for the number of blueberries Avery picked.

Enter your answer in the box.

```



```
Quarts

28. Xavier asked 50 people what their favorite number between 0 and 100 is. He organized the data into intervals below. Use the grid provided to draw a histogram of this data. Be sure to include a title for the graph, label the axes, and select an appropriate scale.

Favorite Numbers	
Number Range	Number of People
1 - 20	18
21 - 40	8
41 - 60	11
61 - 80	12
81 - 100	1

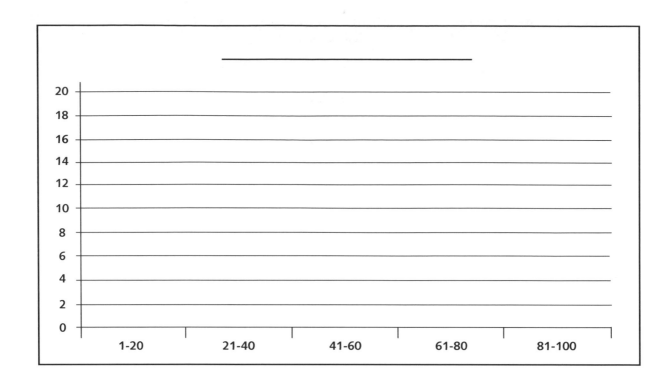

29. The diagram represents 3x + 4.

| 1x |
| 1x |
| 1x |

1
1
1
1

PART A

What is 2(2x + 5) in simplified form?

Enter your answer in the box.

PART B

Using the 1x tile and 1 tile displayed above, show how you arrived at your answer.

Enter your answer in the box.

LumosLearning.com   ▼

30. The student to teacher ratio at Finch Middle School is 17: 1.

<u>**PART A**</u>

If there are 1,476 students and teachers combined at Finch Middle School, how many teachers are there?

Enter your answer in the box.

Teachers

<u>**PART B**</u>

Show or explain how you arrived at your answer.

Enter your answer in the box.

PART - 4

31.   At Woodbridge Middle School's annual concert, for every 2 popular tunes played 3 classical tunes were played, for a ratio of popular to classical of 2: 3.

   PART A

   If they played 10 popular and classical tunes in all, how many classical tunes were played?

   Enter your answer in the box.

	tunes

   PART B

   If the bands played two more classical tunes, what would be the new ratio of popular to classical tunes, in simplest form?

   Enter your answer in the box.

   | |
   | |
   | |

32.   Victoria rolled two six-sided number cubes ten times and recorded the sum of each roll.

   ## 6, 4, 10, 8, 9, 7, 12, 7, 6, 2

   PART A

   Determine the median, first quartile, and third quartile for this set of data.

   Enter your answer in the box.

   | |
   | |
   | |

PART B

Use the above information to create a box-and-whisker plot of the data.

Enter your answer in the box.

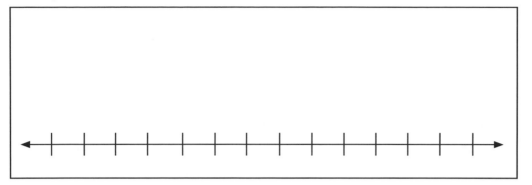

33. If the volume of a sphere is calculated using the formula given below, what is the volume of a sphere with a radius of 2 cm, to the nearest tenth? Use 3.14 for π.

$$V_{sphere} = \frac{4}{3}\pi r^3$$

Enter your answer in the box.

cm²

34. The area of a kiboc is equal to the length of its side squared plus two.

PART A

Write an expression to represent the area, A, of a kiboc in terms of its side, s.

Enter your answer in the box.

PART B

Using the expression, calculate the area of a kiboc with a side length of 7mm.

Enter your answer in the box.

	mm²

35. A partial recipe for Caramel-Vanilla Ice Cream requires 4 cups of sugar, 6 cups of half-and-half, and 3 cups of whipping cream.

PART A

What is the ratio of half-and-half to whipping cream in simplest form?

Enter your answer in the box.

PART B

The recipe makes 3 gallons of ice cream. How many fluid ounces are in 3-gallons?

Enter your answer in the box.

	oz.

PART C

What percentage of the ice cream is sugar, to the nearest percent?

Enter your answer in the box.

	%

LumosLearning.com   ▼

36. Find the quotient. 36,632 ÷ 152 = _____

Enter your answer in the box.

```
┌─────────────────────────────────────────────────────────┐
│                                                           │
│                                                           │
│                                                           │
│                                                           │
└─────────────────────────────────────────────────────────┘
```

37. Nicolas was given the following coordinates and asked to graph them and connect them to form a triangle. A(1,-1) B(-5, -1) C(-5,5). Here is Nicolas' graph.

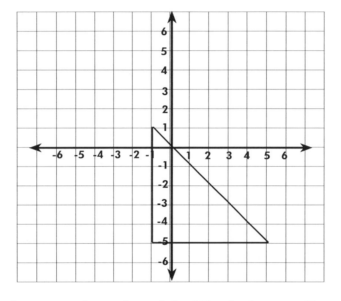

Graph the triangle correctly and explain Nicolas' error. Be specific. Enter your answer in the box.

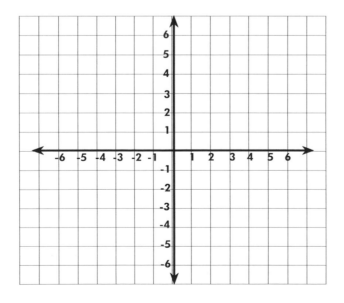

Explain

```



```

38.   Locate the opposite of $\frac{2}{3}$ on the number line.

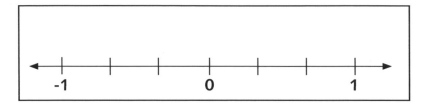

End of Summative Assessment (SA) - 2

▼

Summative Assessment (SA) - 2

Answer Key

Question No.	Answer	Related Lumos Online Workbook	CCSS
PART - 1			
1 Part A	18.75 feet	Solving Real World Ratio Problems	6.RP.3D
1 Part B	225 ft^2	Area	6.G.1
1 Part C	56.52 ft^2	Area	6.G.1
1 Part D	68.34 feet		
2	*	Distribution	6.SP.2
3 Part A	*	Representing Inequalities	6.EE.8
3 Part B	Emilio, Hailey, Tiana	Equations and Inequalities	6.EE.5
4	*	Absolute Value	6.NS.7
5 Part A	$1.79	Unit Rates	6.RP.2
5 Part B	$50.12	Solving Real World Ratio Problems	6.RP.3B
6	A and B	Identifying Equivalent Expressions; Writing Equivalent Expressions	6.EE.4, 6.EE.3
7	1 1/20	Division of Fractions	6.NS.1
8 Part A	A triangular pyramid	Nets	6.G.4
8 Part B	110.4 in^2	Nets	6.G.4
9	*	Representing Inequalities	6.EE.8
10	11.96 m^2	Area	6.G.1
PART - 2			
11	5149	Operations with Decimals	6.NS.3
12 Part A	11.25 minutes	Solving Real World Ratio Problems	6.RP.3B
12 Part B	5.76 kms.	Solving Real World Ratio Problems	6.RP.3B
13 Part A	25 fireflies	Solving Real World Ratio Problems	6.RP.3
13 Part B	5 fireflies	Solving Real World Ratio Problems	6.RP.3
13 Part C	3:2	Expressing Ratios	6.RP.1

* See detailed explanation

Question No.	Answer	Related Lumos Online Workbook	CCSS
14 Part A	$262.50	Positive and Negative Numbers	6.NS.5
14 Part B	$12.50	Positive and Negative Numbers	6.NS.5
15	3n - 5	Expressions Involving Variables	6.EE.2A
16	30.55 cm^2	Area	6.G.1
17 Part A	45 + h ≥ 54	Representing Inequalities	6.EE.8
17 Part B	*	Representing Inequalities	6.EE.8
18 Part A	*	Solving Real World Ratio Problems	6.RP.3A
18 Part B	g = 2d	Quantitative Relationships	6.EE.9
18 Part C	108	Expressions Involving Variables	6.EE.2C
19 Part A	$0.03 or 3 cents	Solving Real World Ratio Problems	6.RP.3B
19 Part B	*	Solving Real World Ratio Problems	6.RP.3B
20 Part A	9	Data Interpretation	6.SP.5C
20 Part B	*	Graphs and Charts	6.SP.4
PART - 3			
21 Part A	1:3	Expressing Ratios	6.RP.1
21 Part B	$1.67 / 1 brownie	Unit Rates	6.RP.2
21 Part C	50%	Solving Real World Ratio Problems	6.RP.3C
22	A & D	Statistical Questions	6.SP.1
23	C	Using Common Factors	6.NS.4
24	17	Whole Number Exponents	6.EE.1
25	8,400	Surface Area and Volume	6.G.2
26 Part A	167 words per minute	Unit Rates	6.RP.2
26 Part B	14.3 minutes	Solving Real World Ratio Problems	6.RP.3B
27 Part A	2x-3=9	Solving One-Step Equations	6.EE.7
27 Part B	*	Solving One-Step Equations	6.EE.7
28	*	Graphs and Charts	6.SP.4
29 Part A	4x+10	Writing Equivalent Expressions	6.EE.3
29 Part B	*	Writing Equivalent Expressions	6.EE.3

* See detailed explanation

LumosLearning.com   ▼

Question No.	Answer	Related Lumos Online Workbook	CCSS
30 Part A	82	Solving Real World Ratio Problems	6.RP.3
30 Part B	*	Solving Real World Ratio Problems	6.RP.3
PART - 4			
31 Part A	6 classical tunes	Expressing Ratios	6.RP.1
31 Part B	1:2	Expressing Ratios	6.RP.1
31 Part A	*	Graphs and Charts	6.SP.4
31 Part B	*	Graphs and Charts	6.SP.4
33	33.5 cm^3	Expressions Involving Variables	6.EE.2C
34 Part A	$A = s^2 + 2$	Whole Number Exponents	6.EE.1
34 Part B	51 mm^2	Whole Number Exponents	6.EE.1
35 Part A	2:1	Expressing Ratios	6.RP.1
35 Part B	384 ounces	Solving Real World Ratio Problems	6.RP.3B
35 Part C	8%	Solving Real World Ratio Problems	6.RP.3C
36	241	Division of Whole Numbers	6.NS.2
37	*	Coordinate Geometry	6.G.3
38	*	Representing Negative Numbers	6.NS.6A

* See detailed explanation

Summative Assessment (SA) - 2

Detailed Explanations

Question No.	Answer	Detailed Explanation
		PART - 1
1 Part A	18.75 feet	There are 12 inches in a foot. Write 9 inches as a fraction over 12 and convert to a decimal. 18 feet 9 inches $= 18\frac{9}{12}$ feet $= 18.75$ feet
1 Part B	225ft²	There area of a rectangle is the length multiplied by the width. Use the width in feet only. $A = l \times w = (12)(18.75) = 225ft^2$
1 Part C	56.52 ft²	The area of a semicircle is half the area of a circle or $\frac{1}{2}\pi r^2$. $A = \frac{1}{2}\pi r^2 = \frac{1}{2}(3.14)(6)^2 = \frac{1}{2}(3.14)(36) = 56.52$ ft²
1 Part D	68.34 feet	The perimeter, shown in dotted line, consists of three sides of the rectangle and the circumference of half a circle. Obtain the circumference of half a circle and add the rectangle sides to find the perimeter. The diameter is equal to 12 feet, $2(6) = 12$. $C = \frac{1}{2}\pi d = \frac{1}{2}(3.14)(12) = 18.84$ feet $18.84 + 2 \times 18.75 + 12 = 68.34$ feet
2		First find the mean median and the mode of the data. Mean: $\dfrac{40 + 14 + 36 + 19 + 32 + 26 + 4 + 15 + 26 + 38}{10} = 25$ Median: 4, 14, 15, 19, 26, 26, 32, 36, 38, 40 = 26 Mode: 26

Statement	True, False, NEI
The mean is less than the mode.	True
The median and the mode are equal.	True
The mode is the middle number.	False
If Charlotte brought in 10 instead of 4, the median would be greater.	False

Question No.	Answer	Detailed Explanation
3 Part A		w≤2:43 m≤2:18
3 Part B	Emilio, Hailey, Tiana	Emilio, Hailey, Tiana: Emilio's time is less than or equal to 2:18 and both Hailey's and Tiana's time is less than or equal to 2:43.
4		When ordering rational numbers in different forms, convert them all to the same form, i.e. fractions, decimals, or percents. I chose to convert them all to decimals. $$0.75 \quad \frac{8}{6} \quad \text{-}50\% \quad \text{-}\frac{15}{3} \quad 0.7 \rightarrow 0.75 \quad 1.3\ldots \quad \text{-}.50 \quad \text{-}5 \quad 0.7$$ Then order the numbers from least to greatest and rewrite them in their original form. $$\text{-}5 \text{-} 0.5 \quad 0.7 \quad 0.75 \quad 1.3\ldots \rightarrow \frac{\text{-}15}{3}, \text{-}50\%, 0.7, 0.75, \frac{8}{6}$$
5 Part A	$1.79	To solve for a unit rate of cost per ice cream sandwich, write the given rate and write an equivalent rate with the denominator of one. $$\frac{\$35.80}{20} = \frac{x}{1}; \$35.80 = 20x; x = \$1.79$$
5 Part B	$50.12	Use the unit rate you found in PART A and multiply by the number of baseball team members $1.79 × 28=$50.12
6	A and D	Ⓐ -10x + 7 – 2x + 11 - when like terms are combined this is equivalent to -12x + 18 Ⓓ -12x + 18 - this is the answer in simplest form
7	$1\frac{1}{20}$	Dividing by a fraction is the same as multiplying by its reciprocal. Be sure to simplify your answer. $$\frac{7}{8} \div \frac{5}{6} = \frac{7}{8} \times \frac{6}{5} = \frac{42}{40} = 1\frac{2}{40} = 1\frac{1}{20}$$
8 Part A	A triangular pyramid	A triangular pyramid
8 Part B	110.4 in²	Find the area of one triangle and, since they are all congruent, multiply by 4. $$A_{triangle} = \frac{bh}{2} = \frac{(8)(6.9)}{2} = 27.6 \text{ in}^2$$ 27.6 x 4=110.4 in²

Question No.	Answer	Detailed Explanation
9		The phrase "at most 20" means the number can be twenty but no greater. The graph Landon drew says the number can be 20 or greater. The correct graph of "at most 20" is below.

The correct number line graph showing "at most 20" with the point at 20 and arrow pointing left.

| 10 | | I do not agree with everything Tristan did. I agree with his calculation for the area of R1, see diagram. Tristan's area for R2 is incorrect. The width is 1.4 m but the height is 2.6 m. Tristan forgot to subtract the width of R1 from 5.2, $5.2 - 2.6 = 2.6$ m. The correct area for R2 and the total area are below. |

$$A_{R2} = (2.6)(1.4)$$
$$A_{R2} = 3.64 \text{ m}^2$$

$$A_{Total} = 8.32 + 3.64$$
$$A_{Total} = 11.96 \text{ m}^2$$

Diagram of L-shaped figure with R2 (height 2.6 m, width 1.4 m) and R1, with measurements 1.8 m, 1.4 m, 5.2 m, 2.6 m, and 3.2 m.

PART - 2

Question No.	Answer	Detailed Explanation
11	5149	$25.745 \div 0.005 = 5149$
12 Part A	11.25 minutes	Since you know the rate of minutes to kilometers, set up a proportion and solve but remember to convert kilometers to meters first. There are 1600 meters in 1.6 kilometers. $\frac{20 \text{ minutes}}{1600 \text{ meters}} = \frac{x \text{ minutes}}{900 \text{ meters}}$; $(20)(900) = 1600x$; $18000 = 1600x$; $11.25 = x$ It will take Aki 11.25 minutes to walk 900 meters.
12 Part B	5.76 kilometers	If it takes Aki 20 minutes to walk 1.5 kilometers, you can set up a proportion to solve for the number of kilometers she can walk in 72 minutes. $\frac{20 \text{ minutes}}{1.6 \text{ km}} = \frac{72 \text{ minutes}}{x \text{ km}}$; $20x = (1.6)(72)$; $20x = 115.2$; $5.76 = x$ Aki can walk 5.76 kilometers in 72 minutes.
13 Part A	25 fireflies	The ratio of fireflies is 3 : 5 : 4, which means 3 parts to 4 parts to 5 parts. This makes a total of $3 + 4 + 5$ or 12 parts. If they caught 60 altogether then one part of 60 is 60/12 or 5 fireflies. If Brandon caught five parts then he caught (5)(5) or 25 fireflies.

Question No.	Answer	Detailed Explanation
13 Part B	5 fireflies	Using the same logic as in PART A, Chet caught four parts and each part is 5 fireflies so Chet caught (4)(5) = 20 fireflies. Nathan caught 3 parts for (3)(5) = 15 fireflies. The difference between the number of fireflies Chet and Nathan caught is 20 − 15 or 5 fireflies.
13 Part C	3:2	If Brandon catches five more fireflies he will have 30 fireflies, 25 + 5. Then the ratio between Brandon and Chet will be 30 : 20 or 3 : 2.
14 Part A	$262.50	Maya spent $250.00 plus an additional $12.50 for a total of $262.50.
14 Part B	$12.50	An account balance of -12.50 means that Maya owes the bank or is in debt to the bank for $12.50.
15	3n - 5	3n - 5
16	30.55 cm^2	To find the area of the pentagon, calculate the area of the rectangle and the triangle and add them together. $$A_{rectangle} = (9.4)(2.1) = 19.74 \text{ cm}^2$$ $$A_{triangle} = \frac{(9.4)(2.3)}{2} = 10.81 \text{ cm}^2$$ $$A_{pentagon} = 19.74 + 10.81 = 30.55 \text{ cm}^2$$
17 Part A	45 + h ≥ 54	
17 Part B		$$45 + h \geq 54$$ $$h \geq 9$$
18 Part A		Dollars: 1.00, **2.00**, 3.00, **4.00**, 5.00 / Golf Balls: **2**, 4, **6**, 8, **10**
18 Part B	g = 2d	g = 2d
18 Part C	108 golf balls	Use the equation in PART B and substitute 54 for d and solve for g. $$g = 2d \; ; \; g = 2(54) \; ; \; g = 108$$ Liwei sold 108 golf balls.

Question No.	Answer	Detailed Explanation
19 Part A	$0.03 or 3 cents	Write a fraction with the cost in the numerator and the number of envelopes in the denominator. Then write an equivalent fraction with the denominator of one. $$\frac{\$14.89}{500 \text{ envelopes}} = \frac{x}{1 \text{ envelope}} ; \$14.89 = 500x \text{ '} \$0.02978 = x$$ The cost per envelope is $0.03 or 3 cents
19 Part B	$1.00	Alan misunderstood that his father wanted the price for one envelope and not the number of envelopes one can buy for $1.00.
20 Part A	9	First order the data: 4, 6, 8, 10, 16, 22 Median: 4, 6, 8, 10, 16, 22 = 9
20 Part B		

Animals at the Zoo

Question No.	Answer	Detailed Explanation
21 Part A	1:3	The cost of a Rice Krispies® treat is $0.50 and the cost of a fruit tart is $1.50, thus the ratio is 0.5 to 1.5 or in simplest form with integers only it is 1 : 3.
21 Part B		If 3 brownies cost $5.00 divide $5.00 by 3 to get the cost of one brownie.
21 Part C	50%	To find the percentage of the cost spent on fruit tarts we must first find the total cost and the amount spent on fruit tart. $$\text{Cost}_{total} = 4(.50) + 4(.25) + 2(1.50) = \$6.00$$ $$\text{Cost}_{fruit\ tart} = 2(1.50) = \$3.00$$ The percentage of the total cost spent on fruit tart is the fraction of the money spent of fruit tarts over the total cost, written as a percent. Fifty percent of the total cost was spent on fruit tart.

Question No.	Answer	Detailed Explanation
22	A and D	Of these questions A and D have answers that vary. Many things depend on how long a dog lives or how many miles you can drive on a gallon of fuel. Questions B & C have answers that are definitive.
23	C	Answer choice C will go evenly into 15 and 6, $15 \div 3 = 5$ and $6 \div 3 = 2$. So $15 + 6$ is the same as $3(5 + 2)$. You can also find the value of each expression and compare. $15 + 6 = 21$ and $3(5+2)$ or $3(7)$ is also 21.
24	17	Remember that an exponent tells you how many times to multiply the base by itself. $3^2 - 2^3 + 4^2 = (3)(3) - (2)(2)(2) + (4)(4) = 9 - 8 + 16 = 17$
25	8,400 cubes	Find the number of ¼ cm cubes that will fit along the length, width, and height of the box. $$7 \div \frac{1}{4} = 7 \times \frac{4}{1} = 28 \text{ cubes}$$ $$6.3 \div \frac{1}{4} = 6.3 \times \frac{4}{1} = 25.2 \text{ cubes, or 25 cubes}$$ $$3.2 \div \frac{1}{4} = 3.2 \times \frac{4}{1} = 12.8 \text{ cubes, or 12 cubes}$$ Then use the volume formula for a rectangular prism to find the total number of cubes the box will hold. $V = l \times w \times h = 28 \times 25 \times 12 = 8,400$ cubes
26 Part A	167 words	Use the words in the problem to help solve the problem. Words per minute means $\frac{words}{minute}$. $$\frac{500 \text{ words}}{3 \text{ minutes}} = \frac{x \text{ words}}{1 \text{ minute}}; 500 = 3x; 167 = x.$$ Sean can type about 167 words per minute.
26 Part B	14.3 minutes	In Part A, you found how many words Sean can type per minute. If you multiply this rate by the number of words, 2,380, you will determine the amount of time it will take to type the document. $$2,380 \text{ words} \times \frac{1 \text{ minute}}{167 \text{ words}} = 14.25 \text{ or } 14.3 \text{ minutes}$$
27 Part A		Chloe picked x quarts and Avery picked x – 3 quarts and when added together they picked 9 quarts. $$x + (x - 3) = 9 \text{ or } 2x - 3 = 9$$

Question No.	Answer	Detailed Explanation
27 Part B		First find put how many quarts Chloe picked by solving for x. Then subtract this number from 9 to determine how many quarts Avery picked. $2x - 3 = 9$; $2x = 12$; $x = 6$ quarts – Chloe picked $9 - 6 = 3$ quarts - Avery picked
28		
29 Part A	$4x+10$	$2(2x+5)=(2)(2x)+(2)(5) = 4x+10$
29 Part B		
30 Part A	82 teachers	$1,476 \div 18 = 82$ teachers
30 Part B		A ratio is a part to part so a ratio of 17 to 1 means 17 parts to 1 part or a total of 18 parts. If 1,476 is divided into 18 parts, each part will contain 82 units. Since the teachers only make up one part there are 82 teachers at Finch Middle School. You can always check your answer by calculating how many in 17 parts, $(17)(82) = 1,394$, and adding it with the other part. The total should equal the total number of students and teachers combined. $1,394 + 82 = 1,476$.

PART - 4

Question No.	Answer	Detailed Explanation
31 Part A	6 classical tunes	The ratio of tunes of 2 : 3 means 2 parts to 3 parts for a total of 5 parts. If they played 10 tunes all together then one part of 10 is 10/5 or 2 tunes. Since 3 parts were classical tunes and there are 2 tunes per part then (3)(2) or 6 classical tunes were played.

     LumosLearning.com   ▼

Question No.	Answer	Detailed Explanation
31 Part B	1:2	If there were 10 tunes all together and six were classical tunes then four were popular tunes. Now, if the bands played two more classical tunes then this would be a total of 2 + 6 or 8 classical tunes. So the ratio of popular tunes to classical tunes would be 4 : 8 or 1 : 2 in simplest form.
32 Part A		Order the numbers: 2, 4, 6, 6, 7, 7, 8, 9, 10, 12 Find the median: 2, 4, 6, 6, 7, 7, 8, 9, 10, 12 = 7 Find Q1, the median of the first half of the data: 2, 4, 6, 6, 7 = 6 Find Q3, the median of the second half of the data: 7, 8, 9, 10, 12 = 9
32 Part B		
33	33.5 cm³	Substitute 2 for r and solve. $V_{sphere} = \frac{4}{3}\pi r^3 = \frac{4}{3}(3.14)(2)^3 = \frac{4}{3}(3.14)(8) = 33.493 = 33.5\ cm^3$
34 Part A	$A = s^2 + 2$	$A = s^2 + 2$
34 Part B	51 mm²	Substitute 7 for s and solve. $A = s^2 + 2 = 7^2 + 2 = 49 + 2 = 51\ mm^2$
35 Part A	2:1	There are 6 cups of half-and-half and 3 cups of whipping cream for a ratio of 6 : 3 or 2 : 1 in simplest form.
35 Part B	384 ounces	There are 4 quarts in a gallon, 2 pints to a quart, 2 cups to a pint, and 8 ounces to a cup. $3\ gallons \times \frac{4\ quarts}{1\ gallon} \times \frac{2\ pints}{1\ quart} \times \frac{2\ cups}{1\ pint} \times \frac{8\ ounces}{1\ cup} = 384\ ounces$
35 Part C	8%	There are 8 ounces in 1 cup so 4 cups of sugar is equal to 32 ounces. The percent of sugar in the ice cream is equal to the fraction of sugar in the ice cream written as a percent. $\frac{32\ ounces\ sugar}{384\ ounces\ of\ ice\ cream} = 0.083 = 8\%$ The ice cream is 8% sugar.
36	241	36,632 ÷ 152 = 241

Question No.	Answer	Detailed Explanation
37		 For each point Nicolas switched the x and y-values. For example the coordinates of Point A are (1,-1) which means x = 1 and y = -1, Nicolas plotted x = -1 and y = 1.
38		

LumosLearning.com

Practice Section

In this section, you will see additional practice questions.

TYPE - 1

1.   Mrs. Guptil is making a blanket with a length of 5.4 feet.

   PART A

   If the blanket will have an area of 34.02 ft², how wide will the blanket be?

   Enter your answer in the box.

   [   ] **Feet**

   PART B

   There will be a 2-foot wide border around the blanket. What is the area of the border?

   [   ] **Feet²**

   PART C

   The border will be made of yellow fabric that costs $1.02 per square foot. How much will the border fabric cost?

   [   ] **$**

2. The table shows x- and y-values.

X	Y
1	3
2	6
3	9
4	
5	

PART A

Complete the table.

PART B

Write an equation to express y in terms of x.

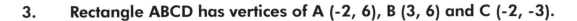

PART C

If the value of x is 103, what is the value of y?

3. Rectangle ABCD has vertices of A (-2, 6), B (3, 6) and C (-2, -3).

PART A

Draw the rectangle on the grid and determine the coordinates of vertex D.

Enter your answer in the box.

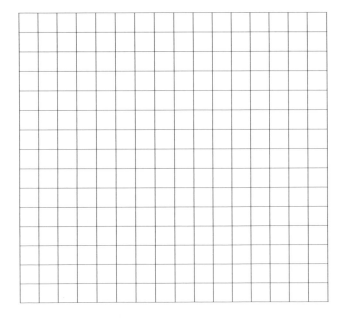

PART B

What is the perimeter of rectangle ABCD?

Enter your answer in the box.

4. If the average of the following data is 8, what is the value of b?

    3, 9, 8, 5, 10, 4, 4, b

    Enter your answer in the box.

5. The diagram shows a net of a 3D figure.

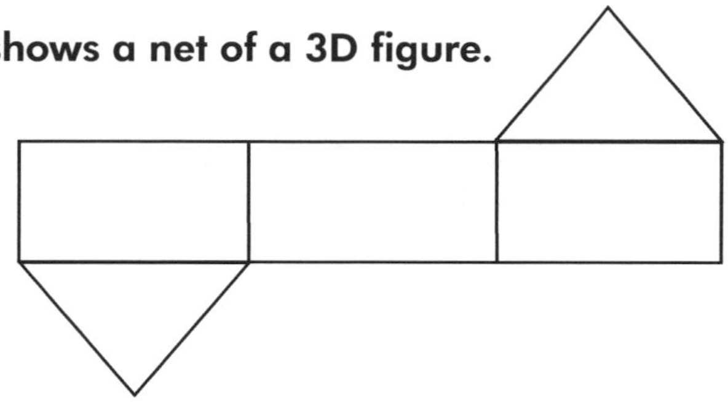

PART A

What figure does this net represent? Be specific.

Enter your answer in the box.

PART B

Each triangle has an area of 6 in^2 and the rectangular region has a length of 12 in. and a width of 4 in. What is the surface area of the net?

Enter your answer in the box.

in^2

6. The following expression represents the school's cost for 6 students to attend an after school event.

$$6\left(\frac{2}{3}x - 10\right)$$

PART A

Simplify the expression using the Distributive Property.

Enter your answer in the box.

```

```

PART B

If x = $125, what is the school's cost for the event?

Enter your answer in the box.

```

```

7. Trenton can prepare 12 packages in 10 minutes. Each package contains 8 bars of soap.

PART A

How many full packages must Trenton prepare for 168 bars of soap?

Enter your answer in the box.

```

```
Packages

PART B

How long will it take Trenton to prepare the number of packages found in Part B?

Enter your answer in the box.

```

```
Minutes

LumosLearning.com

How long does it take Trenton to prepare 1 package?

Enter your answer in the box.

	Minutes

8. Renata and Dylan were raking leaves for their elderly neighbor. Renata raked x piles of leaves and Dylan raked $\frac{2}{3}$ the number of piles that Renata did. Together they raked 15 piles of leaves.

PART A

Write an equation to represent this situation.

Enter your answer in the box.

PART B

Use the equation above to solve for the number of piles Dylan raked.

Enter your answer in the box.

	Piles

PART C

Assuming they maintain this same rate, if Dylan rakes 36 piles of leaves how many piles will Renata have raked?

Enter your answer in the box.

	Piles

9. Harper used $\frac{2}{3}$ of a piece of string that was $\frac{5}{6}$ feet long. How long was the piece of string Harper used?

Enter your answer in the box.

```
┌─────────────────────────────────────────────────────────────────┐
│                                                                   │
│                                                                   │
│                                                                   │
│                                                                   │
│                                                                   │
│                                                                   │
└─────────────────────────────────────────────────────────────────┘
```

10. The diagram shows a sandbox with a length of 6.5 feet, a width of 5.5 feet and a height of 6 in.

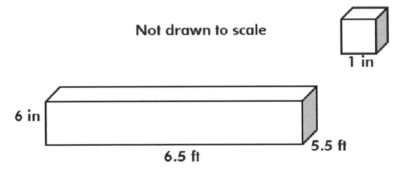

Not drawn to scale

1 in

6 in

6.5 ft

5.5 ft

PART A

What are the length and width of the sandbox in inches?

Enter your answer in the box.

```
┌─────────────────────────────────────────────┐
│                                             │
│                                             │
│                                             │
│                                             │
└─────────────────────────────────────────────┘
```

PART B

How many 1-in cubes will fit in the sand box? Round your answer to the nearest hundredth.

Enter your answer in the box.

```
┌─────────────────────────────────────────────┐
│                                             │
│                                             │
│                                             │
│                                             │
└─────────────────────────────────────────────┘
```

LumosLearning.com

11. **Locate the following numbers on the number line below.**

$$\frac{-1}{2}, \ 100\%, \ 0.2, \ \frac{3}{5}, \ -0.9$$

Enter your answer in the box.

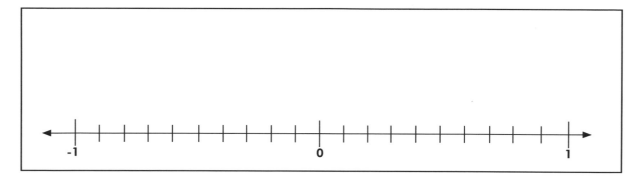

12. **It costs $45.00 for 100 tablets of a joint supplement.**

PART A

How much does one tablet cost?

Enter your answer in the box.

PART B

If one tablet is taken a day, how much does it cost for a year's supply?

Enter your answer in the box.

13. **Mrs. Torchia picked 54 flowers, which represents 60% of all the flowers in her garden. This is shown in the diagram below.**

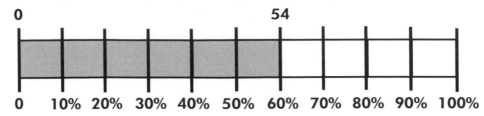

How many flowers are left in Mrs. Torchia's garden?

Enter your answer in the box.

```

```

14. **Jayce went fishing with his father in Lake Travis. It took Jayce 20 minutes to catch a fish. (Assume Jayce can maintain this catching rate.)**

PART A

Write an equation that shows the time, t, it takes to catch f number of fish.

Enter your answer in the box.

```

```

PART B

If Jayce caught 4 fish, how many minutes did it take?

Enter your answer in the box.

```
                                                            min
```

LumosLearning.com

PART C

Jayce's father caught 10 fish in the same amount of time. On average, how many minutes did it take him to catch one fish?

Enter your answer in the box.

	min

15.   Triangle ABC has vertices of A (-1,2), B (2,2) and C (2,6).

PART A

Draw the triangle on the grid.

Enter your answer in the box.

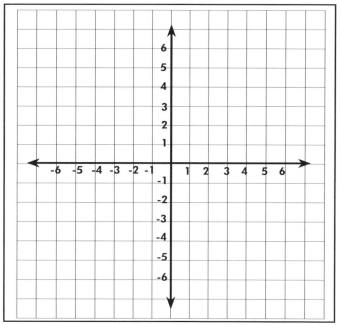

If the length of side AC is 10 inches, what is the perimeter of ΔABC? The distance between grid lines in 2 inches.

Enter your answer in the box.

	inches

16. Which data set below has a mean, median, and mode that are equal?

    Ⓐ 2, 2, 4, 5, 5, 5, 6, 8
    Ⓑ 4, 4, 6, 8, 8, 9, 10, 12
    Ⓒ 10, 11, 14, 14, 15, 16, 18
    Ⓓ 5, 6, 7, 7, 8, 10

17. Gabriela is going to paint a wooden box to hold her treasures. See diagram

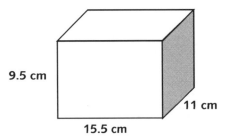

PART A

Draw a net for the box and label the length, width and depth.

Enter your answer in the box.

LumosLearning.com

Part B

Gabriela is going to cover the box in a golden fabric. What is the minimum amount of fabric she will need to cover the box?

Enter your answer in the box.

cm^2

18. Diego works at a vegetable farm and earns $6.00/hour plus $1.25 for every full wagonload of picked vegetables.

PART A

Write an expression to represent how much Diego earns if he works y hours and fills x wagonloads.

Enter your answer in the box.

PART B

If Diego works six hours and fills 20 wagonloads, how much does he earn, to the nearest cent?

Enter your answer in the box.

19. **Olivia opens a bank account and deposits $514.**

   PART A

   During the month Olivia withdraws $120.00 and deposits $40. What is her new balance?

   Enter your answer in the box.

   | | $ |

   PART B

   At the end of each month Olivia earns 0.05% interest on the money in her account. How much interest did she earn this month, to the nearest cent?

   Enter your answer in the box.

   | | $ |

   PART C

   What is the balance of her bank account with the monthly interest?

   Enter your answer in the box.

   | | $ |

20. **Savannah and Claire are making bead jewelry. Claire can assemble twice as many necklaces as Savannah in the same amount of time. Together the girls will make 24 necklaces.**

   PART A

   If Savannah assembled x necklaces, write an equation to model the situation above.

   Enter your answer in the box.

   | |

LumosLearning.com

PART B

Use the equation above to solve for the number necklaces Claire assembled.

Enter your answer in the box.

	Necklaces

PART C

If it took Claire 2 hours to complete the number of necklaces determined in Part B, how long did it take Claire to complete one necklace?

Enter your answer in the box.

	Minutes

21. Mr. Pete made a strawberry rhubarb pie. On the first day half the pie was eaten. How many 1/8 pieces can he make from the remaining half of the pie?

Enter your answer in the box.

22. Billy says the absolute value of -6 is 6. Lisa says, "That can be true because I know that the absolute value of 6 is also 6."

PART A

Who is correct? Show or explain how you got your answer.

Enter your answer in the box.

PART B

Billy lives 7 miles due west of school and Lisa lives 3 miles due east of school. Who lives closer to school? Explain your answer.

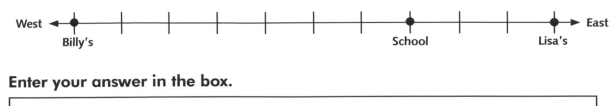

West ←————————————————————————→ East

Billy's · · · · · · · · School · · Lisa's

Enter your answer in the box.

```



```

23. The diagram shows a tall box with a height of x feet, a length of 3.1 feet, and a width of 2.2 ft.

Not drawn to scale

x ft

2.2 ft

3.1 ft

PART A

If the volume of the box is 81.84 ft³, what is the height of the box?

Enter your answer in the box.

```




```

PART B

If three of these boxes are stored side-by-side as in the diagram, how much floor space is needed?

Enter your answer in the box.

```




```

LumosLearning.com   ◀

24. Locate the following numbers on the number line below.

$\dfrac{-1}{4}$ 0.75   10% $\dfrac{-4}{5}$ 0.3

Enter your answer in the box.

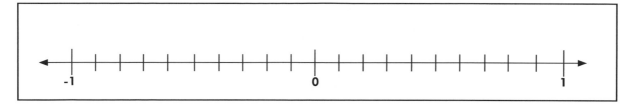

25. Mr. Bade spends an average of $42.50 during a five-day workweek on lunch.

PART A

If he eats every day during his 5-day workweek, what is the average cost for one lunch?

Enter your answer in the box.

PART B

If he started taking lunch to work two days out of five, how much would Mr. Bade save?

Enter your answer in the box.

26. Hoc studied for 2 hours. The first $\frac{1}{4}$ of the time was spent on Social Studies, the next $\frac{3}{8}$ of the time on Spanish and the last $\frac{3}{8}$ of the time on math.

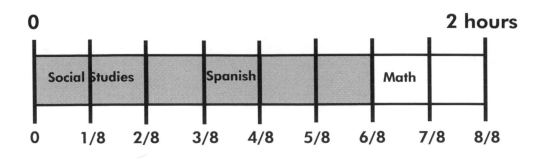

PART A

How long did Hoc spend studying math?

Enter your answer in the box.

	Minutes

PART B

If Hoc spent one-third of his math studying time reviewing flashcards, for how long did he review his flash cards?

Enter your answer in the box.

	Minutes

End of Practice Section

Practice Section

Answer Key

Question No.	Answer	Related Lumos Online Workbook	CCSS
		TYPE - 1	
1 Part A	6.3 ft.	Area	6.G.1
1 Part B	62.8 ft².	Area	6.G.1
1 Part C	$64.06	Solving One-Step Equations	6.EE.7
2 Part A	*	Solving Real World Ratio Problems	6.RP.3A
2 Part B	$y = 3x$	Quantitative Relationships	6.EE.9
2 Part C	$y = 309$	Expressions Involving Variables	6.EE.2C
3 Part A	*	Coordinate Geometry	6.G.3
3 Part B	28 units	Coordinate Geometry	6.G.3
4	$b = 21$	Data Interpretation	6.SP.5C
5 Part A	triangular prism	Nets	6.G.4
5 Part B	60 in²	Nets	6.G.4
6 Part A	4x - 60	Writing Equivalent Expressions	6.EE.3
6 Part B	$440.00	Expressions Involving Variables	6.EE.2C
7 Part A	21 packages	Solving Real World Ratio Problems	6.RP.3
7 Part B	17.5 minutes	Solving Real World Ratio Problems	6.RP.3
7 Part C	50 seconds	Solving Real World Ratio Problems	6.RP.3B
8 Part A	$x + \frac{2}{3}x = 15$	Solving One-Step Equations	6.EE.7
8 Part B	6 piles	Solving One-Step Equations	6.EE.7
8 Part C	54 piles	Solving Real World Ratio Problems	6.RP.3
9	0.55....Feet	Division of Fractions	6.NS.1
10 Part A	L = 78 inches W = 66 inches	Solving Real World Ratio Problems	6.RP.3D
10 Part B	30,888	Surface Area and Volume	6.G.2
11	*	Representing Negative Numbers	6.NS.6C

* See detailed explanation

Question No.	Answer	Related Lumos Online Workbook	CCSS
12 Part A	$0.45	Solving Real World Ratio Problems	6.RP.3B
12 Part B	$164.25	Solving Real World Ratio Problems	6.RP.3
13	36 flowers	Division of Fractions	6.NS.1
14 Part A	t = 20f	Quantitative Relationships	6.EE.9
14 Part B	60 minutes	Expressions Involving Variables	6.EE.2C
14 Part C	6 minutes	Unit Rates	6.RP.2
15 Part A	*	Coordinate Geometry	6.G.3
15 Part B	24 inches	Coordinate Geometry	6.G.3
16	C	Data Interpretation	6.SP.5C
17 Part A	*	Nets	6.G.4
17 Part B	844.5 cm^2	Nets	6.G.4
18 Part A	6y+1.25x	Solving One-Step Equations	6.EE.7
18 Part B	$61.00	Expressions Involving Variables	6.EE.2C
19 Part A	$434.00	Positive and Negative Numbers	6.NS.5
19 Part B	$0.22	Solving Real World Ratio Problems	6.RP.3C
19 Part C	$434.22	Positive and Negative Numbers	6.NS.5
20 Part A	x+2x=24	Solving One-Step Equations	6.EE.7
20 Part B	16 necklaces	Expressions Involving Variables	6.EE.2C
20 Part C	7.5 minutes	Solving Real World Ratio Problems	6.RP.3B
21	4 pieces	Division of Fractions	6.NS.1
22 Part A	Both Billy and Lisa	Absolute Value	6.NS.7C
22 Part B	*	Absolute Value	6.NS.7C
23 Part A	12 ft=x	Surface Area and Volume	6.G.2
23 Part B	20.46 ft^2	Area	6.G.1
24	*	Representing Negative Numbers	6.NS.6C
25 Part A	$8.50	Solving Real World Ratio Problems	6.RP.3B
25 Part B	$17.00	Solving Real World Ratio Problems	6.RP.3
26 Part A	45 minutes	Division of Fractions	6.NS.1
26 Part B	15 minutes	Division of Fractions	6.NS.1

* See detailed explanation

LumosLearning.com

Practice Section

Detailed Explanations

Question No.	Answer	Detailed Explanation
		TYPE - 1
1 Part A	6.3 ft.	A blanket is a rectangle of material. The area of a rectangle is obtained by multiplying the length by the width. If the area is 34.02 ft² this is equal to 5.4 ft. multiplied by x. To obtain the width divide 34.02 ft² by 5.4 ft. A=length × width 34.02=5.4x 34.02=5.4x 6.3 = x The width of the blanket is 6.3 ft.
1 Part B	62.8 ft².	Find the perimeter of the blanket and multiply by the width of the border. $P_{blanket}$=2(5.4)+ 2(6.3)= 10.8+12.6=23.4 feet Then add four 2-foot by 2-foot squares to fill in the 4 corners of the blanket's border. A_{border}=23.4ft × 2ft +4 (2 ft x 2 ft) =62.8 ft² The area of the border is 62.8 ft².
1 Part C	$64.06	Multiply the cost by the square footage found in Part B. 62.8 ft² × $1.02=$64.06

2 Part A

x	y
1	3
2	6
3	9
4	12
5	15
6	18
7	21
8	24

Question No.	Answer	Detailed Explanation
2 Part B	$y = 3x$	Notice that the x-value multiplied by 3 results in the y-value. There for the rule or expression for x in terms of y is $y = 3x$.
2 Part C	$y = 309$	Using the rule above, $y = 3x$, substitute 103 for x and solve for y. $y = 103(3)$; $y = 309$
3 Part A		The coordinates of vertex D are (-3, -3)
3 Part B	28 units	Count the units on the grid to determine the length of each side. Segments AB and DC are 5 units; Segments AD and BC are 8 units. The perimeter $= 5 + 5 + 9 + 9 = 28$ units.
4	$b = 21$	If the average of 8 numbers is 8, the sum of the numbers must be 64. $3 + 11 + 8 + 5 + 10 + 4 + 13 + b = 64$; $43 + b = 64$; $b = 21$
5 Part A	triangular prism	The net represents a triangular prism with two triangles as bases.
5 Part B	60 in²	Find the area of all surfaces and add them together. The area of each triangle is given as 6 in². The area of the rectangular region is: $A_{rectangle} = l \times w = (12)(4) = 48$ in² Now add all the areas together to find the surface area of the net. $A_{total} = 6+6+48 = 60$ in²
6 Part A	4x-60	The 6 must be multiplied by the $\frac{2}{3}x$ and the (- 10) $6\left(\frac{2}{3}x - 10\right) = 4x - 60$
6 Part B	$440.00	Substitute $125 for x in the above equation and solve. $4(125) - 60 = 500 - 60 = \$440.00$

LumosLearning.com ◀

Question No.	Answer	Detailed Explanation
7 Part A	21 packages	Set up a proportion involving packages and soap bars and solve. $\dfrac{1 \text{ packages}}{8 \text{ bars}} = \dfrac{x \text{ packages}}{168 \text{ bars}}$; (1) (168) = 8x; 168 = 8x ; 21 packages
7 Part B	17.5 mins	Set up a proportion involving packages and time and solve. $\dfrac{10 \text{ minutes}}{12 \text{ packages}} = \dfrac{x \text{ minutes}}{21 \text{ packages}}$; (10) (21) = 12x; 210 = 12x ; x = 17.5 minutes
7 Part C	50 seconds	$\dfrac{10 \text{ minutes}}{12 \text{ packages}} = \dfrac{x \text{ minutes}}{1 \text{ package}}$; (10) (1) = 12x ; 10 = 12x ; $\dfrac{10}{12}$ x $\dfrac{10}{12} = \dfrac{5}{6}$ minutes = 50 seconds
8 Part A & B	$x + \dfrac{2}{3}x = 15$	Use the equation in Part A to solve for, the number of piles Renata raked. $x + \dfrac{2}{3}x = 15$; $\dfrac{3}{3}x + \dfrac{2}{3}x = 15$; $\dfrac{5}{3}x = 15$; 5x = (15)(3); 5x = 45 ; x = 9 Since Dylan ranked $\dfrac{2}{3}$x piles, he ranked $\dfrac{2}{3}$(9) or 6 piles
8 Part C	54 piles	To determine the number of piles Renata would rake if Dylan raked 36 piles, find 2/3 of what number is 36. 2/3 x = 36 ; 2x = (3)(36); 2x = 108 ; x = 54 piles
9	0.55... Feet	Find the length of the piece of string Harper used by calculating $\dfrac{2}{3}$ of $\dfrac{5}{6}$ feet. $\dfrac{2}{3} \times \dfrac{5}{6} = \dfrac{10}{18} = \dfrac{5}{9} = 0.55....$ Feet
10 Part A		There are 12 inches in a foot, so multiply the length and the width by 12 to calculate the number of inches. Length:(6.5)(12)= 78 inches Width:(5.5)(12)= 66 inches
10 Part B		Find the number of 1 in. cubes that will fit along the length, width, and height of the box. Length: 78÷1= 78 cubes Width: 66÷1= 66 cubes Depth:6÷1= 6 cubes Then use the volume formula for a rectangular prism to find the total number of cubes the box will hold. V= l×w×h=78 ×66 × 6=30,888 1-in cubes

Question No.	Answer	Detailed Explanation

11

12 Part A — $0.45=x

Write a rate for the cost for 100 tablets and then write an equivalent fraction with one as the denominator.

$$\frac{\$45.00}{100\ tablets} = \frac{x}{1\ tablet}\ ;\ \$45.00 = 100x\ ;\ \$0.45 = x\ ;\ \$0.45 = x$$

12 Part B — $164.25

Use the unit price per tablet and multiply it by the number of days in a year, 365.

$$365 \times \$0.45 = \$164.25$$

13 — 36 flowers

If 54 flowers make up 60% of Mrs. Torchia's garden then 54 ÷ 6 or 9 flowers make up 10% of her garden. She has 40% of her flowers remaining and 4 × 9 = 36. Mrs. Torchia has 36 flowers left in her garden.

14 Part A — t = 20f

t = 20f

14 Part B — 60 minutes

Substitute 4 for f in the equation in Part A.

$$t = 20f = (20)\ (4) = 60\ minutes$$

14 Part C — 6 minutes

Jayce's father caught 10 fish in 60 minutes. To find the unit rate or the number of minutes to catch one fish write an equivalent rate with a denominator of 1 fish.

$$\frac{60\ minutes}{10\ fish} = \frac{x\ minutes}{1\ fish}\ ;\ x = 6\ minutes$$

Jayce's father can catch a fish in 6 minutes.

15 Part A

Question No.	Answer	Detailed Explanation
15 Part B	24 inches	Side AB is 3 units and side BC is 4 units. Since each grid unit is 2 inches, side AB is 6 inches and side AB is 8 inches. Therefore the perimeter of triangle ABC is 6 + 8 + 10 or 24 inches.
16	C	median: 4.625 median: 5 mode: 5 median: 7.625 median: 8 mode: 8 **mean: 14** **median: 14** **mode: 14** mean: 7.16 median: 7 mode: 7
17 Part A		
17 Part B	844.5 cm²	We need to find the surface area of the box by summing the areas of all the surfaces. A=2(9.5)(15.5)+ 2(9.5)(11)+2(11)(15.5) A=294.5 +209+341= 844.5 cm²
18 Part A	6y + 1.25x	Let y = hours worked and y = wagonloads filled. 6y + 1.25x
18 Part B	$61.00	In the equation above, substitute 6 for y and 20 for x. 6(6)+(1.25)(20)= 36+25=$61.00
19 Part A	$434.00	A withdrawal is represented as a negative number. A deposit is represented as a positive number. $514 – $120.00 + $40.00 = $434.00
19 Part B	$0.22	At the end of the month Olivia had a balance of $434.00. To calculate the amount of interest she earned, multiply the balance by 0.0005. $434.00 × 0.0005 = 0.217=$0.22
19 Part C	$434.22	$434.00 x $0.22 = $434.22
20 Part A	24	x + 2x = 24

Question No.	Answer	Detailed Explanation
20 Part B	16 necklaces	$x+2x=24$; $3x=24$; $x=8$ Claire assembled 2x necklaces or $2(8) = 16$ necklaces.
20 Part C	7.5 mins	Write a fraction to represent the rate for 16 necklaces and then find the unit rate or rate for one necklace. Two hours is 120 minutes. $$\frac{120 \text{ minutes}}{16 \text{ necklaces}} = \frac{x \text{ minutes}}{1 \text{ necklace}} ; 120 = 16x ; 7.5 = x$$ It took Claire 7.5 minutes to assemble one necklace.
21	4 pieces	Find the answer by dividing $1/2$ by $\frac{1}{8}$ $$\frac{1}{2} \div \frac{1}{8} = \frac{1}{2} \times \frac{8}{1} = \frac{8}{2} = 4 \text{ pieces}$$
22 Part A		Both Billy and Lisa are correct. The absolute value of a number is the distance that number is from 0 on the number line. Both 6 and -6 are six units from zero and hence have the same absolute value.
22 Part B		Lisa lives closer since she is only 3 miles or 3 units from school. Billy lives farther away because he lives 7 miles or 7 units away from school. There is no negative distance.
23 Part A	12 ft=x	Use the volume formula and substitute the known values to solve for the height. $$V = l \times w \times h$$ $$81.84 = (3.1)(2.2)(x)$$ $$81.84 = 6.82(x)$$ $$12 \text{ ft} = x$$
23 Part B	20.46 ft²	The floor space is the area filled by the bottom of the boxes. Find the area of one box bottom and multiply by three. $$A = l \times w$$ $$A = 3.1 \times 2.2$$ $$A = 6.82 \text{ ft}^2$$ The floor area filled by the three boxes is $(6.82)(3) = 20.46 \text{ ft}^2$

Question No.	Answer	Detailed Explanation
24		
25 Part A	$8.50	$\dfrac{\$42.50}{5} = \$8.50$
25 Part B		If he took lunch twice a week he would only need to buy lunch three times a week. So (3)($8.50) = $25.50. This will save him $42.50 - $25.50 = $17.00.
26 Part A	45 minutes	There are 120 minutes in 2 hours. 120 divide by 8 is 15 minutes. If each unit in the bar above is 15 minutes. Then Hoc spent (3)(15) or 45 minutes studying math.
26 Part B	15 minutes	Looking at the bar for this question, the math section is already divided into three equal parts. Since each part is 15 minutes. Hoc spent 15 minutes reviewing his flashcards.

Lumos StepUp™ is an educational app that helps students learn and master grade-level skills in Math and English Language Arts.

The list of features includes:

- Learn Anywhere, Anytime!

- Grades 3-8 Mathematics and English Language Arts

- Get instant access to the Common Core State Standards

- One full-length sample practice test in all Grades and Subjects

- Full-length Practice Tests, Partial Tests and Standards-based Tests

- 2 Test Modes: Normal mode and Learning mode

- Learning Mode gives the user a step-by-step explanation if the answer is wrong

- Access to Online Workbooks

- Provides ability to directly scan QR Codes

- And it's completely FREE!

http://lumoslearning.com/a/stepup-app

lumoslearning

INCLUDES Online Workbooks!

About Online Workbooks

* When you buy this book, 1 year access to online workbooks is included

* Access them anytime from a computer with an internet connection

* Adheres to the Common Core State Standards

* Includes progress reports

* Instant feedback and self-paced

* Ability to review incorrect answers

* Parents and Teachers can assist in student's learning by reviewing their areas of difficulty

Course Name: Grade 4 Math Prep

Lesson Name:	Correct	Total	% Score	Incorrect
Introduction				
Diagnostic Test		3	0%	3
Number and Numerical Operations				
Workbook - Number Sense	2	10	20%	8
Workbook - Numerical Operations	2	25	8%	23
Workbook - Estimation	1	3	33%	2
Geometry and measurement				
Workbook - Geometric Properties		6	0%	6
Workbook - Transforming Shapes				
Workbook - Coordinate Geometry	1	3	33%	2
Workbook - Units of Measurement				
Workbook - Measuring Geometric Objects	3	10	30%	7
Patterns and algebra				
Workbook - Patterns	7	10	70%	3
Workbook - Functions and relationships				

LESSON NAME: Workbook - Geometric Properties

Elapsed Time: 01:19

Question No. 2

What type of motion is being modeled here?

Select right answer

◯ a translation
◯ a rotation 90° clockwise
◉ a rotation 90° counter-clockwise
◯ a reflection

[Previous question]   [Next question]

Report Name: Missed Questions

Student Name: Lisa Colbright
Cours Name: Grade 4 Math Prep
Lesson Name: Diagnostic Test

The faces on a number cube are labeled with the numbers 1 through 6. What is the probability of rolling a number greater than 4?

Answer Explanation

(C) On a standard number cube, there are six possible outcomes. Of those outcomes, 2 of them are greater than 4. Thus, the probability of rolling a number greater than 4 is "2 out of 6" or 2/6.

A)		1/6
B)		1/3
C)	Correct Answer	2/6
D)		3/6

Lumos Learning
Developed By Expert Teachers

6 Grade

PARCC 2016
Practice Tests
ENGLISH LANGUAGE ARTS

- ☆ **2** Summative Assessments
- ★ Additional Practice Passages
- ★ Includes access to the Mobile Apps
- ★ Answer Key and Detailed Explanations

tedB∞k

PLUS **Online Workbooks**
With Hundreds of Practice Questions

Adheres to Common Core State Standards
www.LumosLearning.com

Available
- At Leading book stores
- Online www.LumosLearning.com

48732032R00060

Made in the USA
Lexington, KY
11 January 2016